CW00336230

SCOTLAND'S NEW WRITING THEATRE    T

Traverse Theatre Company and Ieatr Polski Bydgoszcz

# Cherry Blossom

Written by Catherine Grosvenor
in collaboration with Lorne Campbell,
Mark Grimmer and Leo Warner

cast in alphabetical order

Sandy Grierson
John Kazek
Marta Ścisłowicz
Małgorzata Trofimiuk

| | |
|---|---|
| Director | Lorne Campbell |
| Dramaturg | Łukasz Chotkowski |
| Set Designer | Leo Warner |
| Video Designers | Fifty Nine Productions |
| Lighting Designer | Sergey Jakovsky |
| Sound Designer | Alasdair Macrae |
| Costume Designer | Sarah Holland |
| Assistant Designer | Henry Broadhurst |
| Voice and Dialect Coach | Ros Steen |

| | |
|---|---|
| Stage Manager | Gemma Smith |
| Deputy Stage Manager | Vicky Wilson |
| Assistant Stage Manager | Dan Dixon |
| AV and Sound Operator | Jonathon Lyle |

**First performed at the Traverse Theatre**
**Wednesday 24 September 2008**

**a Traverse Theatre Commission**

# TRAVERSE THEATRE

### Artistic Director: Dominic Hill

## A Rolls-Royce machine for promoting new Scottish drama across Europe and beyond.
(The Scotsman)

The Traverse's commissioning process embraces a spirit of innovation and risk-taking that has launched the careers of many of Scotland's best-known writers including John Byrne, David Greig, David Harrower and Liz Lochhead. It is unique in Scotland in that it fulfils the crucial role of providing the infrastructure, professional support and expertise to ensure the development of a dynamic theatre culture for Scotland.

## The importance of the Traverse is difficult to overestimate . . . without the theatre, it is difficult to imagine Scottish playwriting at all. (Sunday Times)

From its conception in the 1960s, the Traverse has remained a pivotal venue in Edinburgh. It receives enormous critical and audience acclaim for its programming, as well as regularly winning awards. Alan Wilkins' commission for the Traverse, *Carthage Must Be Destroyed*, won Best New Play at the 2008 Critics' Awards for Theatre in Scotland. From 2001–07, Traverse Festival productions of *Gagarin Way* by Gregory Burke, *Outlying Islands* by David Greig, *Iron* by Rona Munro, *The People Next Door* by Henry Adam, *Shimmer* by Linda McLean, *When the Bulbul Stopped Singing* by Raja Shehadeh, *East Coast Chicken Supper* by Martin J Taylor, *Strawberries in January* by Evelyne de la Chenelière in a version by Rona Munro and *Damascus* by David Greig have won Fringe First or Herald Angel awards (and occasionally both). In 2008 the Traverse's Festival programme *Manifesto* picked up an incredible sixteen awards including a record seven Scotsman Fringe Firsts and four Herald Angels.

## The most ambitious playwriting on the Edinburgh Festival Fringe. (New York Times)

The Traverse's success isn't limited to the Edinburgh stage. Since 2001, Traverse productions of *Gagarin Way, Outlying Islands, Iron, The People Next Door, When the Bulbul Stopped Singing*, the *Slab Boys Trilogy, Mr Placebo* and *Helmet* have toured not only within Scotland and the UK, but in Sweden, Norway, the Balkans, Germany, USA, Iran, Jordan and Canada. Immediately following the 2006 festival, the Traverse's production of *Petrol Jesus Nightmare #5 (In the Time of the Messiah)* by Henry Adam was invited to perform at the International Festival in Priština, Kosovo, and won the Jury Special Award for Production. During spring 2008, the Traverse toured its award-winning 2007 production of *Damascus* to Toronto, New York and Moscow.

**The Traverse has done Edinburgh proud.** (The Observer)

The Traverse's work with young people is of supreme importance and takes the form of encouraging playwriting through its flagship education project *Class Act*, as well as the Young Writers' Group. *Class Act* is now in its 18th year and gives school pupils the opportunity to develop their plays with professional playwrights and work with directors and actors to see the finished piece performed on stage at the Traverse. This year, for the fourth year running, the project also took place in Russia. The hugely successful Young Writers' Group is open to new writers aged 18 – 25 with fortnightly meetings led by a professional playwright. This Autumn the Traverse will, for the first time, work with young men from HM Young Offenders Institution Polmont to improve their literacy skills through practical drama and playwriting in a project called *OutWrite*. The participants will work with theatre professionals to develop their own plays which will be performed both at HM YOI Polmont and at the Traverse.

**The Traverse has an unrivalled reputation for producing contemporary theatre of the highest quality, invention and energy, and for its dedication to new writing.**
(Scotland on Sunday)

The Traverse is committed to working with international playwrights and in 2005 produced *In the Bag* by Wang Xiaoli in a version by Ronan O'Donnell, the first ever full production of a contemporary Chinese play in the UK. This project was part of the successful Playwrights in Partnership scheme, which unites international and Scottish writers, and brings the most dynamic new global voices to the Edinburgh stage. Other international Traverse partnerships have included work in Québec, Norway, Finland, France, Italy, Portugal and Japan.

To find out about ways in which you can support the work of the Traverse please contact our Development Department 0131 228 3223 or development@traverse.co.uk
www.traverse.co.uk

## TEATR POLSKI BYDGOSZCZ

### Artistic Director: Pawel Lysak

Teatr Polski in Bydgoszcz is one of the most distinguished theatres in Poland. The theatre has a wide-ranging repertoire which includes contemporary drama, alongside reinterpretations of classic Polish texts and international plays. The theatre programmes its work on a thematic basis, including public meetings, discussions, and installations to accompany their core productions. Their repertory ensemble company brings together directors, theatre practitioners and actors who are committed to creating political theatre characterised by radical statements. The theatre regularly presents work internationally, touring to other venues and festivals.

www.teatrpolski.pl

# COMPANY BIOGRAPHIES

### Henry Broadhurst (Assistant Designer)

Henry trained at Gray's School of Art and at the Digital Design Studio, Glasgow School of Art, specialising in 3D design and 3D motion graphics. He is an Associate Designer of Fifty Nine Productions, with whom he has worked on *125th Anniversary Gala* (Metropolitan Opera New York); *Alex the Stage Play* (Arts Theatre, UK and international tour); Matthew Bourne's *Dorian Gray* (New Adventures); *Sinatra* (international tour); *Kabaret SQ*, *Sweet Fanny Adams in Eden* (Stellar Quines Theatre Company). Henry has also created animations for the Royal Botanic Garden Edinburgh, Pure Magic Films, Malcolm Fraser Architects and Absolute Studios.

### Lorne Campbell (Director)

Lorne was Associate Director at the Traverse from 2005 to 2008. Directing credits for the Traverse include the world premières of *Night Time* by Selma Dimitrijevic, *Carthage Must Be Destroyed* and *The Nest* by Alan Wilkins, *Distracted* by Morna Pearson, *White Point* by David Priestly, *Broke* by David Lescot in a version by Iain F MacLeod, *Melody* by Douglas Maxwell and *In the Bag* by Xiaoli Wang in a version by Ronan O'Donnell. Lorne was also Associate Director for *East Coast Chicken Supper* by Martin J Taylor and *The People Next Door* by Henry Adam (Balkan tour 2004). Other theatre credits include: *How to Tell the Monsters from the Misfits* (Birmingham Rep); *Brokenville* (British Council/ Young Audience's Ensemble of Togliatti); *The Dumb Waiter, Death and the Maiden, An Evening with Damon Runyon, A Comedy of Errors, As You Like It, Journey's End* (Forge Theatre); *The Chairs* (RSAMD); *The Cheviot, The Stag and the Black, Black Oil* (Taigh Chearsabhagh).

### Łukasz Chotkowski (Dramaturg)

Łukasz is Chief Dramaturg at Teatr Polski in Bydgoszcz. He has worked as a dramatist on *The Glass Menagerie* (Teatr Współczesny, Szczecin); *Sprawa Dantona* [*The Danton Case*] (Teatr Polski, Bydgoszcz). Łukasz directed the Polish premiere of Elfriede Jelinek's new play *Über Tiere* [*About Animals*] and the theatre installation *40KG Do It Yourself Part 1* at Teatr Polski, Bydgoszcz (2008). He has worked as an assistant director for Maja Kleczewska on *Fedra* (Teatr Narodowy, Warsaw 2007). He has also written four plays: *Performance of the Butterfly, FromNoHere, The Girl with No Hands* and *Burning My Lips*. *FromNoHere* will be published in the forthcoming *Anthology of New Polish Drama* (Seagull Books: Calcutta, London, New York 2008). He has also published texts on Marina Abramovic and Sarah Kane. Łukasz was Curator of the Polish-German Theatre Festivals *Express EC 47 – Shades and Shadows of Politics* (2006) and *Post Drama Project* (2005).

## Fifty Nine Productions (Video Designers)
## Leo Warner (Set Designer)
Leo Warner and Mark Grimmer are the founding directors of Fifty Nine Productions, a film and new media production company which specialises in film-making and integrating the moving image into live performance. The company's team plays both a creative and technical role in the realisation of film, theatre, opera, ballet and fine art projects. Leo and Mark are Associate Artists of the National Theatre. Recent stage productions include Matthew Bourne's *Dorian Gray* (New Adventures); *...some trace of her*, *War Horse*, *Attempts on Her Life*, *Waves* (National Theatre); *The Minotaur*, *Salome* (Royal Opera House); *Satyagraha* (Metropolitan Opera/ENO); *Alex the Stage Play* (Arts Theatre, UK and international tour); *Carmen* (ENO); *7 Deadly Sins* (Royal Ballet); and *Black Watch* (National Theatre of Scotland). Forthcoming projects include *Dr Atomic* (Metropolitan Opera/ENO); The Metropolitan Opera's *125th Anniversary Gala*; *Dido and Aeneas* (ENO/Young Vic); and *Request Programme* (Schauspiel, Cologne).

## Sandy Grierson (Performer)
Sandy trained under David W W Johnstone of Lazzi (with whom he has performed in *Oresteia*, *Witkacy: Idiota* and *Mr Pinocchio*). He also studied with Zofia Kalinska of Ariel Teatr, Poland, playing in *The Night of the Great Season*, *A Little Requiem for Kantor* and *Dybbuk*. Sandy is an Artistic Associate of Vanishing Point and has appeared in *Little Otik* (co-production with the National Theatre of Scotland), *Subway*, *Mancub*, *Lost Ones*, *Stars Beneath the Sea* and *Invisible Man*. Other theatre credits include *The Wizard of Oz* (Royal Lyceum, Edinburgh); *Fergus Lamont* (Communicado Theatre); *James and the Giant Peach*, *Charlotte's Web* (Citizens' Theatre); *Home* (National Theatre of Scotland); *The Privately Personal Lives of Dorian Gray* (Cumbernauld Theatre); *An Oak Tree* (News from Nowhere); *Romeo and Juliet*, *Sunset Song* (Prime Productions); *A Christmas Carol* (Wee Stories); *Hair of the Dog* (Intoto Productions); *Tam O'Shanter* (Puppet Lab); and *The Soul of Chien-Nu-Leaves Her Body* (Young Vic).

## Catherine Grosvenor (Writer)
Catherine was born in Edinburgh and studied German and Polish at Cambridge University. Her first play, *One Day All This Will Come to Nothing*, was produced by the Traverse in 2005. Her play *Lucky Lady* was commissioned by Sweetscar and premiered at the Tron Theatre in March 2007 as part of the *Sure Shots* series. *Cherry Blossom* is her second full-length play.

## Sarah Holland (Costume Designer)

Sarah recently graduated from Telford College with an HND in Theatre Costume. Previous Wardrobe credits with the Traverse include *Fall* and *Nova Scotia*. Sarah has also worked at the Traverse on *Damascus*, *Petrol Jesus Nightmare #5 (In the Time of the Messiah)* and *Melody*. Originally from Cork, she has worked with Irish companies such as Cork Opera House, Everyman Theatre and Corcadorca.

## Sergey Jakovsky (Lighting Designer)

Sergey was born in St Petersburg, Russia, and trained in Technical and Production Arts at RSAMD. He has a long-term association with kinetic theatre company Sharmanka and is the lighting and sound designer for all of their new work, exhibitions and theatrical collaborations. Design credits for Sharmanka include *Wheels of Life*, *Endgame*, *Druid's Clock*, *Movement and Shadow*, *Sharmanka Exhibition* and *The Millennium Clock Tower*. Other theatre credits include *We Dance Wee Groove* (Still Motion/Starcatchers); *The Drawer Boy*, *A Boy's Own Story* (Tron Theatre); *Blank Album*, *Bunty and Doris*, *Madame Bazie* (Gilmore Productions); *Lost Happy Endings* (Botanic Productions); *73 and a Half Minutes* (Company Chordelia); *Robert's Dream* (Derevo Theatre); *How to Steal a Diamond* (Vox Motus); *Memories of Earth*, *Adventures of Baron*, *Baron's Ball* (The Working Party); *Plain Speaking*, *Soul Pilots* (ek Performance); *My Old Man* (Magnetic North); *Black Sun Over Genoa* (Theatre Workshop); *Hoops, Hats and Acrobats*, *Chrysalids* (Complete Productions); *Carmen* (Haddo House Opera); *Rescuers Speaking* (Birds of Paradise).

## John Kazek (Performer)

John trained at RSAMD. For the Traverse: *Night Time*, *Gorgeous Avatar*, *I was a Beautiful Day*, the *Slab Boys Trilogy*, *Solemn Mass for a Full Moon in Summer* (Traverse/Barbican), *King of the Fields*, *Perfect Days* (Traverse/Vaudeville), *Passing Places*, *Chic Nerds*, *Stones and Ashes*, *Europe*. Other theatre includes *Zarraberri*, *Limbo*, *Sea Change* (Oran Mor); *Tamburlaine Must Die* (Glasgay!/Tron Theatre); *Hamlet*, *Pleasure and Pain*, *Glue*, *A Midsummer Night's Dream* (Citizens' Theatre); *Fergus Lamont* (Communicado/Perth Theatre); *Frozen* (Rapture Theatre); *Cyrano de Bergerac* (Catherine Wheels); *Roam* (Grid Iron/National Theatre of Scotland); *1974 – The End of the Year Show* (Lyric Theatre, Belfast); *Knives in Hens* (TAG Theatre Company); *Hedda Gabler*, *Macbeth*, *Thebans*, *Uncle Vanya*, *'Tis a Pity She's a Whore* (Theatre Babel); *Word for Word* (Magnetic North); *Marabou Stork Nightmare* (Citizens' Theatre/Leicester Haymarket Theatre); *Variety* (Grid Iron); *The Big Funk* (The Arches); *Penetrator* (Tron Theatre); *Mary Queen of Scots, Kidnapped* (Royal Lyceum Theatre, Edinburgh); *Twilight Shift* (7:84 Theatre Company); *Wuthering Heights*, *Driving Miss Daisy* (Byre Theatre);

*King Lear, As You Like It* (Oxford Stage Company). Television credits include *The Key* (BBC/Little Bird); *Auf Wiedersehen, Pet, City Central, Double Nougat, Rab C Nesbitt, Punch Drunk, Strathblair* (BBC); *Taggart, High Road* (STV). Film credits include *The Clan* (Clan Films); *Batman Begins* (Warner Bros); *Dear Frankie* (Scorpio Films Ltd); *How D'Yae Want tae Die* (Dead Man's Shoes Ltd); *Young Adam* (Hanway Films); *Riff Raff* (Parallax Pictures); *Silent Scream* (Antonine Productions).

### Alasdair Macrae (Sound Designer)

Alasdair trained in Theatre Arts at Langside College, Glasgow. He is a Creative Associate of Vanishing Point, with whom he has worked on a number of shows. He was composer, musical director and performer for *Lost Ones*, performed and played live in *Invisible Man*, and was composer and musical director for *Subway*, in which the live performance of a seven-piece Kosovan band was integral to the production. He has also worked with Borderline, Hopscotch, the Tron, Mischief La-Bas, the Traverse, the Arches, the Kings Theatre Glasgow, Take Two Productions and National Theatre of Scotland. Alasdair also has a busy career as a professional musician.

### Marta Ścisłowicz (Performer)

Marta is from Poland and graduated last year from the National Higher School of Theatre in Wrocław. In her final year she made her stage debut at Teatr Polski, Wrocław, in *Don Juan Wraca Z Wojny* [*Don Juan Returns From the War*]. Since July 2007 she has been a company member of Teatr Polski in Bydgoszcz, where she has appeared in *Motortown, Sprawa Dantona* [*The Danton Case*] and *Über Tiere* [*About Animals*]. Film credits include *Jutro idziemy do kina* [*We Are Going To The Cinema Tomorrow*]; *Among Others* (TV Theatre); David Hare's *Przesilenie* [*The Vertical Hour*]. Radio credits include *Obora* [*The Barn*].

### Ros Steen (Voice and Dialect Coach)

Ros trained at RSAMD and has worked extensively in theatre, film and TV. For the Traverse: *The Pearlfisher, Damascus, Night Time, Carthage Must Be Destroyed, strangers, babies,* the *Tilt* triple bill, *Gorgeous Avatar, Melody, I was a Beautiful Day, East Coast Chicken Supper, The Found Man, In the Bag, Shimmer, The Nest,* the *Slab Boys Trilogy, Dark Earth, Homers, Outlying Islands, The Ballad of Crazy Paola, The Trestle at Pope Lick Creek, Heritage* (2001 and 1998), *Among Unbroken Hearts, Shetland Saga, Solemn Mass for a Full Moon in Summer* (as co-director) *King of the Fields, Highland Shorts, Family, Kill the Old Torture Their Young, Chic Nerds, Greta, Lazybed, Knives in Hens, Passing Places, Bondagers, Road to Nirvana, Sharp Shorts, Marisol, Grace in America.* Other theatre credits include *Black Watch, Mancub, Miss Julie*

(National Theatre of Scotland); *Desire Under the Elms, The Bevellers, Shadow of a Gunman, No Mean City, Whatever Happened To Baby Jane?* (Citizens' Theatre); *Romeo and Juliet, Playhouse Creatures, Sweet Bird of Youth, The Talented Mr Ripley, The Graduate* (Dundee Rep); *Little Otik* (Vanishing Point/National Theatre of Scotland); *The Wall* (Borderline); *Resurrection* (Oran Mor); *The Wonderful World of Dissocia* (Edinburgh International Festival/Drum Theatre Plymouth/Tron Theatre); *The Rise and Fall of Little Voice* (Visible Fictions); *Perfect Pie* (Stellar Quines); *The Small Things* (Paines Plough); *My Mother Said I Never Should* (West Yorkshire Playhouse); *Blindsight, Myths of the Near Future* (Untitled); *Singles Night, Little Ones, Home, Transatlantic, The Hanging Tree, Laundry, Entertainment Angels* (LookOUT); *A Taste of Honey, Knives in Hens, Stroma, Sunset Song, A Midsummer Night's Dream* (TAG); *Beneath You – Spider Girls are Everywhere* (Birds of Paradise); *Seeing Voices* (Solar Bear); *Beul Nam Breug* (Tosg Theatar Gaidhlig). Film credits include *Greyfriars Bobby* (Piccadilly Pictures); *Gregory's Two Girls* (Channel4 Films). Television credits include *Sea of Souls, Rockface, 2000 Acres of Skye, Monarch of the Glen, Hamish Macbeth* (BBC).

## Małgorzata Trofimiuk (Performer)
Małgorzata trained at the Bialystok branch of Warsaw Higher School of Theatre. Since 1999 she has been a company member of Teatr Polski in Bydgoszcz. In 2001 and 2004 she won awards for performance in leading roles during Poland's International Theatre Day. Małgorzata has performed Molière, Shakespeare, Ionesco, Elton and Głowacki. Most recently she appeared in Teatr Polski's *Sprawa Dantona* [*The Danton Case*].

# SPONSORSHIP AND DEVELOPMENT

We would like to thank the following
corporate funders for their support

To find out how you can benefit
from being a Traverse Corporate Funder,
please contact our Development Department
on 0131 228 3223 / development@traverse.co.uk

## The Traverse would like to thank
## the members of the Development Board:

Stewart Binnie, Adrienne Sinclair Chalmers, Stephen Cotton,
Paddy Scott and Ian Wittet

## The Traverse Theatre's work
## would not be possible without the support of

**For their continued generous support of Traverse
productions, the Traverse thanks:**
The Pier, 104 George Street, Edinburgh;
Habitat;
Camerabase


**For their help on *Cherry Blossom* the Traverse thanks:**
Royal Lyceum Theatre, Edinburgh, and the
Private Rented Housing Panel


**The Traverse Theatre receives
financial assistance from:**
The Barcapel Foundation, The Binks Trust, The Calouste
Gulbenkian Foundation, The Canadian High Commission,
The Craignish Trust, The Cross Trust, The Cruden Foundation,
Gouvernement de Québec, James Thom Howat Charitable Trust,
The Japan Foundation, The John Thaw Foundation,
The Lloyds TSB Foundation for Scotland, The Misses Barrie
Charitable Trust, The Moffat Charitable Trust,
The Peggy Ramsay Foundation, Ronald Duncan Literary
Foundation, Sky Youth Action Fund, Tay Charitable Trust,
The Thistle Trust, The Weatherall Foundation

www.traverse.co.uk

To find out about ways in which you can support the work of the Traverse
please contact our Development Department 0131 228 3223 or
development@traverse.co.uk

## ARE YOU DEVOTED?

### Our Devotees are:

**Joan Aitken, Stewart Binnie, Katie Bradford, Adrienne Sinclair Chalmers, Adam Fowler, Anne Gallacher, Keith Guy, Iain Millar, Helen Pitkethly, Michael Ridings, Bridget Stevens, Walton & Parkinson, Joscelyn Fox, Gillian Moulton, John Knight OBE**

The Traverse could not function without the generous support of our patrons. In March 2006 the Traverse Devotees was launched to offer a whole host of exclusive benefits to our loyal supporters

### Become a Traverse Devotee for £29 per month or £350 per annum and receive:

- A night at the theatre including six tickets, drinks and a backstage tour
- Your name inscribed on a brick in our wall
- Sponsorship of one of our brand new Traverse 2 seats
- Invitations to Devotees' events
- Your name featured on this page in Traverse Theatre Company scripts and a copy mailed to you
- Free hire of the Traverse Bar Café (subject to availability)

Bricks in our wall and seats in Traverse 2 are also available separately. Inscribed with a message of your choice, these make ideal and unusual gifts.

To join the Devotees or to discuss giving us your support in another way, please contact our Development Department on 0131 228 3223 / development@traverse.co.uk

Charity No. SC002368

# TRAVERSE THEATRE – THE COMPANY

# CHERRY BLOSSOM

Catherine Grosvenor

*in collaboration with*
Lorne Campbell, Mark Grimmer and Leo Warner

'My father reads the dictionary every day.
He says your life depends
on your power to master words.'

*Arthur Scargill*

## Contents

**Foreword**

*Cherry Blossom* was born of two desires: firstly, to explore an alternative commissioning model through which the Traverse Theatre can support and interact with writers creating text through a collaborative process; and secondly, to create a piece of theatre sounding the social phenomenon which has seen upwards of 40,000 Poles arrive in Edinburgh alone since Poland joined the EU in 2004.

The aim of this production is neither journalistic nor exhaustive. We have tried to suggest and wonder, rather than to describe and to define the experiences of a wave of people who have moved from a country with a long and complex history of emigration to a country with a long and complex history of emigration.

The printed text of *Cherry Blossom* should be seen as the written element of a production, rather than as a stand-alone work of fiction and non-fiction. There are three distinct strands: the story of Grażyna Antkiewicz, which presents fiction as truth; the story of the final hours of Robert Dziekanski's life, which edits and presents factual information in the public domain; and selected quotes from some of the many people interviewed during the play's development process.

It has been quite a journey to gather and to make the script, we hope you enjoy it.

*Lorne Campbell and Catherine Grosvenor*

## Acknowledgements

Creating *Cherry Blossom* involved a long period of research and development, both in Scotland and in Poland. Each person we talked to contributed to the mass of ideas, stories and perspectives that formed the basis of the piece. We were struck again and again by the readiness of the Polish people we met to share their experiences with us and to offer their help to us.

We would like to extend particularly warm thanks to: Aneta Prasał-Wiśniewska and her team at the Adam Mickiewicz Institute in Warsaw; Paweł Potoroczyn; Roy Cross; Romuald Poślednik in Bydgoszcz; Jarek Gasiorek of edinburgh.com.pl; and Agneiszka Kwapień and everyone at Polish Art Scotland. A particular mention must also go to Paweł Łysak, without whom the project would not have been possible.

We would like to thank the following people for sharing their time, stories and knowledge with us: Anna Babula, Gemma Bentley, Goshka Bialek, Fr Krzysztof Biernat, Agnieszka Bresler, Maks Bochanek, Karol Chojewski, Roy Cross, Marek Dominiczak, Maciej Dokurno, Lynnette Ferguson, Grażyna Fremi, Radek Gasiorek, Jarosław Giziński, Elwira Grossman, Kasia Gruca, Piotr Gruszczynski, Piotr Hermanowski, Philip Howard, Violeta Ilendo (and Jim), Patrycja Izdebska, Kasia Jagodzinska, Jowita Kaminska, Augustyn Karolewski, Aga Karasiewicz, Anna Kerth, Arek Kozak, Iwona Krasodomska-Jones (and Zosia and Neil), Aneta Kyzioł, Mark Lazarowicz, Emilia Lewandowska, Moore McCartney, Julia and Derek McDonald, Ryszard Maciołek, Katarzyna Mańka, Marta Moskal, Ewa Nagraba, Angelika Neumann, Dorota Ostrowska, Piotr Płachtański, Joe Rosiejak, Marek Rybarczak, Adam Sidor, Ksenia Siedlicka, Filip Sosenko, Teresa Straczynski and everyone at the Polish-Ukrainian Support Group, Krystyna Szumelukowa, Aneta Szyłak, Joe Tarnowski, Colm Wilson, Ewa Winnicka, Ola and Zosia Wojtkiewicz, Matt Zajac and Anika, Gosia and everyone at the Canongate Centre.

If we have omitted or misspelt your name – we apologise and promise to buy you a drink.

*L.C. and C.G.*

## Characters

GRAŻYNA ANTKIEWICZ, *forty-three, a housewife*
PAWEŁ ANTKIEWICZ, *forty-five, a mechanic*
EWA ANTKIEWICZ, *seventeen, in her last year at school*
JASIEK ANTKIEWICZ, *twelve, at school*

MARIA, *the Virgin Mary*

JOHN MCINTYRE, *forty-four, an Edinburgh councillor*

BUS PASSENGERS
ATTENDANT *at Edinburgh Bus Station*
WORKERS *at the Job Centre*
MEAT TEAM *at a pig-processing plant*
LANDLORD
GRAŻYNA'S CLIENTS

*In the original production, all the characters were played by four actors.*

*This text went to press before the end of rehearsals and so may differ slightly from the play as performed.*

**Scene One**

*4th February 2007*

*Exchange rate: £1 = 5.9245 PLN*

*Bydgoszcz, Poland. The Antkiewicz home. The living room.*

GRAŻYNA. How long have you known?

PAWEŁ. I checked it yesterday.

GRAŻYNA. It was there yesterday?

*Silence.*

Was it there yesterday?

EWA. I don't believe this.

PAWEŁ. I just thought, you know, all right, it's not there, it'll be somewhere else.

GRAŻYNA. So it wasn't there? You checked yesterday and it wasn't there and you didn't tell me?

PAWEŁ. It's got to be here somewhere. We still have two hours till the bus goes. We just have to look.

EWA. It's not here!

GRAŻYNA. We have searched the entire flat. We've searched it twice. Every pocket, every drawer, every envelope, every crack. It's not here.

JASIEK. I crawled under my bed, I checked right behind the back legs and behind the wallpaper.

PAWEŁ. I can still travel. I'm still a legal citizen. Legal EU citizen.

GRAŻYNA. It's an international border. They're not going to let you over without any form of ID.

JASIEK. You can get the train, Dad! Dad! Get the train!

PAWEŁ. If I got a new one –

EWA. What else are you going to do?

PAWEŁ. It won't take me that long, I'll just call the factory in England and say I'll be there next week –

GRAŻYNA. Next week? You can't get a new ID in a week.

EWA. Try a month, Dad.

PAWEŁ. I can go in a month then.

GRAŻYNA. In a month? A month? What are we going to live off for a month?

PAWEŁ. We have enough for the rent.

GRAŻYNA. We have enough for the rent as long as no one wants to eat.

EWA. Oh my God.

PAWEŁ. I'm going to go. I'll manage. I'll think of something.

GRAŻYNA. What are we going to do?

PAWEŁ. Antek might have me back.

JASIEK. Or you could fly. Get the plane, Dad. You could get the plane.

GRAŻYNA. You've just quit. He was pleased you quit. He said there's not really enough work for you anyway.

PAWEŁ. He'll have me back if I explain.

GRAŻYNA. And the bus. What about the bus? 250 złoty. 250. For the mercy of God.

PAWEŁ. I'll think of something.

EWA. How can you lose your ID? How can anyone lose their ID?

PAWEŁ. It's easy! What do you need your ID for anyway?

GRAŻYNA. To leave the country! To go abroad and earn money!

EWA. How could you be so stupid?

PAWEŁ. I've just put it in a different place and I just need to remember where I put it. Is that stupid?

EWA. Please. You're not going to remember. You don't have a fucking clue.

GRAŻYNA. Don't talk to your father like that.

EWA. It's true! He doesn't have a clue! We can search this flat for the next two years and we'll never find it. You probably lost it last year. You probably flushed it down the toilet or chucked it in the bin or opened the window and chucked it at the pigeons. 'Hello, pigeons, here's a silly scrap of paper I don't need, would you like to shit on it?'

GRAŻYNA. Ewa, that's enough.

PAWEŁ. I've arranged this whole thing so we have enough money to send you to your special fancy private university. I'm going to work for you and you call me an idiot?

EWA. Everyone else manages, Dad. Everybody else manages to keep their ID in their wallet, everyone else manages to buy a ticket and leave the country, everyone else. Just you. Cos you're an idiot.

PAWEŁ. You've turned into an arrogant bitch, do you know that?

EWA. At least I'm not a loser.

PAWEŁ. I am working to save this family! Where's your gratitude?

EWA. What have I got to be grateful for? He's ruined my life.

GRAŻYNA. Don't be ridiculous.

EWA. I don't want to turn into a housewife just like you, thanks very much.

JASIEK. If you fly, Dad, if you fly with a plane –

PAWEŁ. Shut up, Jasiek.

JASIEK. If you fly they won't check your passport!

GRAŻYNA. Of course they'll check his passport!

EWA. You're such a dumbass.

JASIEK. If he flies, they won't –

GRAŻYNA. He doesn't even have a passport! Don't you understand, Jasiek? No passport, no ID, nothing!

EWA. Get it through your tiny brain, Jasiek, he's not going anywhere.

PAWEŁ. I'm going!

EWA. How?

JASIEK. You can fly!

GRAŻYNA. Get out of here! Get out! I don't want to see you! I don't want to hear you! Get out!

JASIEK. I hate you all!

JASIEK *gets out*.

PAWEŁ. Right. Let's all calm down and think.

GRAŻYNA. Oh God, what are we going to do?

EWA. Okay. Listen. I've got it. I'll get a job.

PAWEŁ. You're not getting a job till you finish your matura.

EWA. I can work weekends. Babysitting.

GRAŻYNA. That's not going to pay the rent.

PAWEŁ. I can borrow Tadziek's! That's a great idea! He even looks like me.

EWA. Now you want to take someone else's ID?

PAWEŁ. He looks like me.

EWA. I don't believe I'm hearing this.

PAWEŁ. No one will notice.

EWA. Of course they'll notice! There is an international border guard, right? They will notice and they will put you in prison for being a total idiot who tried to leave the country with his best friend's ID. For God's sake.

PAWEŁ. Well, what else are we going to do?

GRAŻYNA. I'll go.

PAWEŁ. What?

EWA. What?

GRAŻYNA. I'll go.

PAWEŁ. Go where?

GRAŻYNA. To England.

PAWEŁ. You can't do that.

GRAŻYNA. Why not?

PAWEŁ. Grażyna…

EWA. You?

GRAŻYNA. Someone needs to go. The bus is paid for. We need the money. My ID is valid.

EWA. If someone else goes, it should be me.

GRAŻYNA *and* PAWEŁ. You stay at school.

EWA. You don't even speak English, Mum.

GRAŻYNA. I can speak English.

EWA. No you can't.

GRAŻYNA. I can learn.

PAWEŁ. There's no way you're going.

GRAŻYNA. I don't have a job. Maybe you can go back to Antek. Find another garage. I have nothing.

PAWEŁ. Darling, no. It's impossible.

GRAŻYNA. Why? It makes total sense.

PAWEŁ. What will you do?

GRAŻYNA. Find a job.

PAWEŁ. But what?

GRAŻYNA. Something. Anything. I can clean, I can wash dishes, I can work in a factory.

EWA. You can't go, Mum.

GRAŻYNA. Your father can't go. I can go.

EWA. Mum – look at you. What would you do? You can't go.

PAWEŁ. It's too dangerous. You don't know anyone, you don't know the language...

GRAŻYNA. If everyone else can manage, then so can I. You said yourself. 7,000 złoty for building.

PAWEŁ. You can't be a builder!

GRAŻYNA. A cleaner! 7,000 złoty for cleaning. I can do that. Anyone can do that. For 7,000 złoty, I can do anything.

EWA. Let me go.

PAWEŁ *and* GRAŻYNA. No.

PAWEŁ. You're going to study and go to university. That's what all of this is about. .

EWA. I don't have to go to the Wyższa Szkoła. I can go to the uni. I don't have to go this year. I can get a job.

GRAŻYNA. You're going to the Wyższa Szkoła, and if that means I have to leave tonight to go and clean in England, then that's what I'm going to do.

PAWEŁ. Grażyna. You can't.

GRAŻYNA. Why are you all telling me I can't? You can't. You can't. Jasiek certainly can't. I'm the only one who can.

## Scene Two

*4th February 2007*

*Exchange rate: £1 = 5.9245 PLN*

GRAŻYNA *on the shore. Behind her – land. In front of her – the ocean.*

GRAŻYNA. Holy Mary, Mother of God! Pray for me now and at the hour of my death!

MARIA, *the Virgin Mary, hears that her child is calling her and hurries to her.*

MARIA. My child.

GRAŻYNA. Blessed Virgin!

MARIA. What has happened?

GRAŻYNA *sobbing in fear.*

My child. Shh… Sh… Come to me. Sh…

GRAŻYNA. Help me!

MARIA. Sh…

GRAŻYNA. Holy Mary, I can't, please, let me go home.

MARIA. My child. All is well. I am with you.

GRAŻYNA. Sweet Mary, Mother of God.

MARIA. I am here. All is well. Do you hear me?

GRAŻYNA. I hear you. I love you. Holy Mary, what am I doing?

MARIA. You are embarking on a journey.

GRAŻYNA. I'm going to drown.

MARIA. You will not drown.

GRAŻYNA. I'm going back.

MARIA. You cannot go back.

GRAŻYNA. Look at me! I'm nobody. I'm nothing. What am I going to do? Me? Me? I can't go, I can't do this, what am I going to do, I can't do this I can't leave I can't I can't I have to go back please take me back please –

MARIA. Grażyna. Stop. Take my hand. Close your eyes.

GRAŻYNA. Don't leave me, don't leave –

MARIA. Hold on to me and breathe.

GRAŻYNA *holds her hand and breathes*.

All is well. I am with you. I am always with you.

GRAŻYNA. Always?

MARIA. Breathe…

GRAŻYNA. Holy Mary, I am weak.

MARIA. I am strength.

GRAŻYNA. Yes. Yes. You give me strength. Through you I am strong.

MARIA *sighs*.

Holy Mary –

MARIA. Yes?

GRAŻYNA. Holy Mary, what am I doing?

MARIA. You are going to save your family.

GRAŻYNA. But how?

MARIA. That will come to you.

GRAŻYNA. What can I do? Me?

MARIA. That will come to you.

GRAŻYNA. What if it doesn't?

MARIA. Have faith and all will be well.

GRAŻYNA. I have faith.

MARIA. Then all will be well.

GRAŻYNA. I'm pathetic, I'm weak –

MARIA. You are strong. I am with you. All will be well.

GRAŻYNA. Will it?

MARIA. If you have faith.

GRAŻYNA. I'm abandoning my children.

MARIA. Abandoning them?

GRAŻYNA. I won't be there when they wake up tomorrow, I won't be there to kiss them goodnight, I won't be there when they're hungry, I won't be there when they need help, when they need guidance...

MARIA. You are leaving them quite alone?

GRAŻYNA. Of course not. With their father.

MARIA. Well then.

GRAŻYNA. It's not the same.

MARIA. No.

GRAŻYNA. I can't leave them.

MARIA *rolls her eyes.*

Am I a bad mother? Tell me, Blessed Virgin, tell me.

MARIA. You are doing this for your children, Grażyna. You are a good mother. They will love you and bless you.

GRAŻYNA. They'll hate me.

MARIA. You are a good mother, Grażyna. Your children will love and bless you.

GRAŻYNA. Holy Mary, is that the truth?

MARIA. I am truth.

GRAŻYNA. Yes. Yes, you are.

MARIA. Trust me and all will be well.

GRAŻYNA. All will be well.

MARIA. You will go. You will discover. And all will be well.

GRAŻYNA. May I ask for your blessing?

MARIA. I will be with you every step of the way.

GRAŻYNA. And my children?

MARIA. I will watch them.

GRAŻYNA. Watch Ewa for me. She's so young but she thinks she's so old.

MARIA. I will watch her.

GRAŻYNA. And my Jasiek. My little Jasiek.

*Pause.* GRAŻYNA *looks out at the water.*

It's so vast.

MARIA. It's the ocean. The ocean is unendingly vast.

GRAŻYNA. I'll be lost.

MARIA. You will find your way.

GRAŻYNA. Vast, empty, cold, black.

MARIA. There is so much out there, my child. Go. Go and seek it.

GRAŻYNA. I can't.

MARIA. Go.

## Scene Three

*7th February 2007*

*Exchange rate: £1 = 5.8591 PLN*

*Edinburgh Bus Station.*

PASSENGER 1. Aye, and I says to him, 'Don't know who you think I am, pal, but that's no' the way we do things round here...'

PASSENGER 2. But the X95 is much quicker! The 60 goes via Peebles, I don't want to go to Peebles...

GRAŻYNA. Excuse me.

PASSENGER 3. Paul! Paul! Cheese and Onion or Salt and Vinegar?

PASSENGER 4. Just sit down and be quiet. Where's your colouring book? At Daddy's? Well, it's no use to anyone at Daddy's, is it?

GRAŻYNA. My name is Grażyna. My name is Grażyna.

PASSENGER 5. Can't leave that there, pal, I don't make the rules, I just do as I'm told, and you're going to have to move that.

PASSENGER 6. There's one at 18:25 but there's no' another one till 19:30, unless we got the Dundee bus and changed at Crieff, I don't even know if it stops at Crieff, hold on, naw I cannae see...

GRAŻYNA. Excuse me. Where are the jobs?

PASSENGER 7. And then he's like, 'Oh, it's always my fault, you never think it might be anything to do with you,' and I was like, 'Excuse me? Now it's my fault that we're ten grand in debt and some raging lunatic from Dumbiedykes is trying to track me down and kill me?'

PASSENGER 8. There's no way! £18.00! No way! Listen, just get here, eh? There is no way.

GRAŻYNA. Excuse me. Where is my house?

PASSENGER 9. Totally outrageous. Against every policy we have. Totally outrageous. Yes, you can quote me.

PASSENGER 10. Briiiiiiiiiiiii-aaaaaaaaaaannnnnn! Briiiiiiiiiiiiiiii-aaaaaaaaaaaaaannnnnn!

PASSENGER 11. 'Scuse me, son. 'Scuse me. I've got an awful problem wi' ma ticket. It's ma glasses, ken. Can you have a wee look and tell me which bus I've to get? It's ma glasses. God bless you, son. God bless you.

EWA. You know if you don't get a job we're going to starve to death and I'll never go to uni and it'll just be a total disaster and I'll hate you for ever and ever and ever?

PASSENGER 12. Hi! We need to go to 'Aviemore', is that the name of it, 'Aviemore'? How do we do that? We have the map right here. Do you have the map? Thank you so much!

PASSENGER 13. For fuck's sake! For *fuck's sake*! Twenty-three fucking past, I told you to be here at fucking eleven, not twenty-three fucking past, twenty-three fucking past! What are we going to do now? How could you be such a dick? Twenty-three fucking past!

GRAŻYNA. Paweł? Sweetheart! I miss you. Let's go home. You were right. I can't do it, I just can't. Paweł?

PASSENGER 14. Yeah, I want to see you too, of course I do. You know I do. But it was just such a stressful weekend and I'm absolutely shattered and I really just need to get home and get everything sorted and be in a dark place where there are no children and no animals and no other people at all in fact. No, I'm in Barcelona next week.

PASSENGER 15. How fuckin' brilliant was that goal, by the way? Did ye? Aye, wi' Geggsie, I says to him, 'That man's fuckin' made ae magic, by the way, made ae magic!' See this season, by the way, we're gonnae be fuckin' flying through it, by the way, fuckin' flying.

GRAŻYNA. Jasiek! What are you doing? Get into bed this second! You have school tomorrow and you promised me you were going to be good and work hard. Give me a good-night kiss.

ATTENDANT. Station's closed now. You're going to have to leave.

GRAŻYNA. Yes?

ATTENDANT. We're closed. You have to get out.

GRAŻYNA. Yes?

ATTENDANT. Out!

GRAŻYNA. Out.

Welcome to Edinburgh Bus Station.

A-E Gates F-G.

Way Out. Stance One. *Biały. Wszystko biały.* White.

Night. *Noc*, night. *Zimno*. Cold.

Car. House. Str… strig. *Nie*, street. Car, street, house. Night. Cold.

Bus. Suitcase. Shoes. Woman. Hello. Hello, my name is Grażyna. Where is the house? Where is the job?

**Scene Four**

*8th February 2007*

*Exchange rate: £1 = 5.8416 PLN*

*At the Job Centre.*

WORKER 1. Fill in this form.

WORKER 2. And we'll see what we can do for you.

GRAŻYNA. 'Name, address, date of birth, telephone, e-mail, previous employment, main responsibilities, reason for leaving.'

WORKER 2. All right there?

WORKER 1. Understand the form?

GRAŻYNA. Please?

WORKER 1. Do you understand the form?

GRAŻYNA. Yes, yes.

WORKER 2. You Polish?

GRAŻYNA. Me? Polish? Yes.

WORKER 2. Imye, nazwisko, adres, prasa. Dobshe?

GRAŻYNA. Please?

WORKER 1. Too tie pod pea satch.

WORKER 2. Where do you want to work?

GRAŻYNA. Administration. Childcare. Secretarial. Industrial. Catering and Service.

WORKER 2. Cleaning? Aw, what's cleaning again?

WORKER 1. Spshont-something.

WORKER 2. Spontachka.

WORKER 1. Spontachka! That's the one! You want to spontachka?

WORKER 2. Or fabrica. Factory, you like fabrica?

GRAŻYNA. *Fabryka? W fabryce? Jest praca?*

WORKER 1. Let's put down cleaning and factory.

WORKER 2. Lapdancing-ka?

GRAŻYNA. Please. Job tomorrow?

WORKER 2. Oh, here we go.

WORKER 1. Job tomorrow is difficult. Probably not. Maybe Monday.

GRAŻYNA. Monday?

WORKER 1. Monday, aye.

GRAŻYNA. Today Monday.

WORKER 1. Next Monday.

GRAŻYNA. Next?

WORKER 1. Ken – next week.

GRAŻYNA. One week?

WORKER 1. Aye.

GRAŻYNA. No. Job tomorrow.

WORKER 2. 'Job tomorrow'! I love it!

WORKER 1. Leave your form with us and we'll get back to you, Mrs – random assortment of consonants.

WORKER 2. Dobshe?

**Scene Five**

*15th February 2007*

*Exchange rate: £1 = 5.8093 PLN*

GRAŻYNA *is reading her job document.*

GRAŻYNA. 'Title of job: Factory Line Worker. Job description: Processing and – ' pfft! 'Start date: 16/02/05. Employee name: Grazyna Antkiwic.' Ha! 'Employee name: Grazyna Antkiwic! Start date: 16/02/05!' Me! My job! My start date!

*She takes out her mobile phone and dials home.*

'Mobile phone.'

Hello?

PAWEŁ. Sweetheart, is that you?

EWA. Mum!

JASIEK. Mum!

GRAŻYNA. I've got a job!

EWA. She's got a job?

JASIEK. She's got a job.

PAWEŁ. Doing what?

GRAŻYNA. In a factory.

EWA. How much?

JASIEK. What kind of factory?

PAWEŁ. How much?

GRAŻYNA. £5.35. That's 35 złoty.

PAWEŁ. What kind of factory?

GRAŻYNA. Something with cardboard. Cardboard boxes.

PAWEŁ. She says in a box factory.

JASIEK. Like in *The Simpsons*?

EWA. When do you start?

GRAŻYNA. Yesterday. I already started. Already earning.

MEAT TEAM 1. Workers! Take your pigs.

GRAŻYNA *looks round, bewildered. The pig-processing team are starting up.*

EWA. And what's it like?

MEAT TEAM 1. Open up your pig!

MEAT TEAM 2. Opening up my pig!

PAWEŁ. And you found a place to stay? And you're all right?

GRAŻYNA. Everything's fine.

MEAT TEAM 3. Scald your pig.

MEAT TEAM 1. Grazina! No phones on the factory floor!

MEAT TEAM 2. First cut –

TEAM 1 *and* 3. Saws ready!

MEAT TEAM 2. Grazina! Saw ready!

GRAŻYNA. I have to go – I love you.

TEAM. Cut!

GRAŻYNA. Cut? *Poczekaj! Ja…*

MEAT TEAM 2. First cut – behind the leg.

TEAM. Scrape it all off!

Into the sausage bin.

Backbone – cut.

MEAT TEAM 2. You there! Cut!

TEAM. Saw.

All the way through.

GRAŻYNA. *Ale gdzie?* Where? *Proszę pana!* Excuse –

TEAM. Shoulder.

Gristle. Cut out.

Head.

MEAT TEAM 2. Grażyna! Get that head off, now!

GRAŻYNA. Head! Head *głowa. Głowa* head. *Ale co mam zrobic z głową?*

TEAM. Cut loose.

GRAŻYNA. Cut loose.

Good?

TEAM. Into the sausage bin.

These bits –

We don't need these bits –

Trim and chuck.

GRAŻYNA. Chim and tuck.

TEAM. Into the sausage bin.

Loin – cut.

MEAT TEAM 1. Bacon team!

TEAM 2 *and* 3. Yes!

MEAT TEAM 1. Stand by to slice.

MEAT TEAM 3. Chop team!

MEAT TEAM 1. Yes!

*They all look at* GRAŻYNA.

GRAŻYNA. *Ja?* I?

MEAT TEAM 3. Chop team?

MEAT TEAM 1. Yes!

GRAŻYNA. Yes.

MEAT TEAM 3. Stand by to slice.

TEAM. Cut, cut, cut, cut.

Pack, pack, pack, pack.

£5.35 an hour.

Yes!

£42.80 a shift.

Yes!

Who's for overtime?

Yes!

Health?

Yes!

Safety?

Always!

MEAT TEAM 2. Is there a problem?

GRAŻYNA. Me? No! No problem!

MEAT TEAM 1. You're not pulling your weight.

MEAT TEAM 3. Don't you want the job?

GRAŻYNA. Yes! Of course.

MEAT TEAM 2. So get your act together.

MEAT TEAM 3. Pull your socks up.

MEAT TEAM 1. Get your back into it.

GRAŻYNA. Socks? Back?

MEAT TEAM 2. Workers! Take your pigs!

GRAŻYNA. *Poczekaj, poczekaj, niech ktoś mi powie co mam zrobić.*

MEAT TEAM 2. Take your pigs!

MEAT TEAM 1. Here. Take this one.

GRAŻYNA. This one?

MEAT TEAM 2. Open up your pig!

TEAM 1 *and* 3. Opening up our pigs!

MEAT TEAM 1. Like this.

GRAŻYNA. Open?

MEAT TEAM 2. No talking on the factory floor!

MEAT TEAM 1. Hold your saw like this.

TEAM. Saws ready!

GRAŻYNA. Ready!

MEAT TEAM 1. Think of it like a hot knife through butter.

TEAM. First cut!

GRAŻYNA. First cut.

MEAT TEAM 1. That's it.

TEAM. Scrape all this away.

Into the sausage bin.

GRAŻYNA. Sausage bin.

TEAM. Backbone!

GRAŻYNA. Cut! All the way through! Hot knife of butter!

TEAM. Good job, Grazina!

GRAŻYNA. Me?

MEAT TEAM 1. Yes, you! Good job, Grazina!

GRAŻYNA. Good job, Grażyna!

MEAT TEAM 2. Good worker, Greeza!

MEAT TEAM 3. Good worker, Gina!

MEAT TEAM 1. First hour, Gazina. £5.35.

GRAŻYNA. £5.35!

MEAT TEAM 3. First shift over, Grażyna. How do you feel?

GRAŻYNA. *Czterdzieści dwa funty,* fourfuf two pounds in my
    pocket. Happy.

MEAT TEAM 2. First week over, Grażyna. How do you feel?

GRAŻYNA. Hundred nine seven pound twelve twenty!

MEAT TEAM 1. Before tax.

GRAŻYNA. £197.20! 1,425 złoty! 1,425 zloty in one week.
    Did you hear? Earned by me. Grażyna Antkiewicz, forty-
    three, previous employment history: nothing; previous life
    experience: nothing. 1,425 złoty!

MEAT TEAM 2. And overtime next week.

GRAŻYNA. 1,425 złoty in one week and overtime next week. Rent paid on flat 33/16 Lubińska. Electricity paid on flat 33/16 Lubińska. 400 zloty saved for first installment of fees for BA in Business and Marketing at illustrious Wyższa Szkoła, Bydgoszcz, for Antkiewicz, Ewa.

JASIEK. When are you coming home, Mum?

GRAŻYNA. Hourly rate £5.50? – I'm coming home very soon, darling, just as soon as I can, I miss you. Excuse me? There is mistake. Pay me too much.

MEAT TEAM 1. Finished your three-month probationary period, haven't you? You're a Level One Employee now. Level One hourly rate is £5.50.

GRAŻYNA. Level One Employee. New hourly rate £5.50. £203.50. Before tax but before overtime. Only £7.39 spent on groceries this week. £300 into university fund.

EWA. £300 are 2,000 złoty! 2,000 złoty is half the fee. Oh my God, I'm going to the Wyższa Szkoła. Oh my God.

GRAŻYNA. £50.00 –

PAWEŁ. 350 złoty –

GRAŻYNA. For groceries, household goods and occasional treats for all three inhabitants of flat 33/16 Lubińska, Bydgoszcz.

PAWEŁ. Sweetheart, listen –

EWA. I need a laptop. Tell her I need a laptop.

PAWEŁ. I've been thinking. I think we should all come over.

GRAŻYNA. All of you?

PAWEŁ. Me and Jasiek. When Ewa starts uni she can go into halls and we'll come over.

JASIEK. England! England! England!

GRAŻYNA. You're coming? Really?

PAWEŁ. Absolutely.

EWA. I'm going to my manicure. Laptop.

GRAŻYNA. I can get you a job in the factory.

PAWEŁ. I did some sums. If we're both earning £5.50 an hour –

GRAŻYNA. You start on £5.35.

PAWEŁ. Whatever, if we're both earning that, and that's a lot of money –

GRAŻYNA. When are you coming?

PAWEŁ. In the summer. We'll get a school for Jasiek –

GRAŻYNA. I might be Level Two by then. Level Two is £5.80 an hour.

PAWEŁ. We'll get a school for Jasiek and we'll both be at the factory, we'll get a nice flat –

JASIEK. I'm not going to go to school, I want to work in the factory too.

GRAŻYNA. I can start looking now.

PAWEŁ. And if we sell this place –

JASIEK. Dad, tell her I want to work in the factory too.

GRAŻYNA. Sell what?

PAWEŁ. I've got it all worked out. We sell this place and give the money to Ewa.

GRAŻYNA. You want to sell the flat? Our flat?

PAWEŁ. And give the money to Ewa. We could pay all her fees at once if we sold the flat.

JASIEK. Can I talk now? Can I talk now?

GRAŻYNA. But, Paweł, if we sell the flat –

PAWEŁ. I'm going to get an estate agent to come round. Viewing, it's called.

GRAŻYNA. Sweetheart, if we sell the flat, where are we going to go when we come back?

PAWEŁ. We'll build a new place!

JASIEK. Dad.

PAWEŁ. Hold on, Jasiek wants a word, shall I pass you over?

GRAŻYNA. Of course. But, Paweł, the flat –

PAWEŁ. Don't worry! I've got it all under control! Love you! Here's Jasiek, oh shit, it's beeping at me, you might only have a minute left – Jasiek, take it –

GRAŻYNA. Darling? Darling, how are you?

*The money has run out. The line is dead.*

JASIEK. Mum, Dad didn't tell you. When we come over, I don't want to go to school. I'm going to get a job.

GRAŻYNA. Darling? Hello?

JASIEK. Hello? Mum?

**Scene Six**

*3rd July 2007*

*Exchange rate: £1 = 5.5715 PLN*

JASIEK *and* GRAŻYNA *on the phone.*

JASIEK. Can we fly, Mum? I want to fly.

GRAŻYNA. Of course you can fly.

JASIEK. Will you book the tickets?

GRAŻYNA. Your father can book them.

JASIEK. I think you should book them. In case he books the wrong plane.

GRAŻYNA. You can't book the wrong plane.

JASIEK. No?

GRAŻYNA. Of course not! A plane is a plane.

JASIEK. We might go to the wrong place.

GRAŻYNA. Even your father would struggle to book a ticket for the wrong city.

JASIEK. We could end up in Hawaii. Or New York.

GRAŻYNA. You're coming to Edinburgh and that's that.

JASIEK. It would be so cool if we went to New York by mistake.

GRAŻYNA. You are coming to Edinburgh and that is that.

JASIEK. Or Limerick. Could we go to Limerick?

GRAŻYNA. Where's Limerick?

JASIEK. I don't know.

GRAŻYNA. Why do you want to go there then?

JASIEK. That's where Bartek's going. His whole family.

GRAŻYNA. Is it in England?

JASIEK. Bartek and Maciej and his mum and his dad. Now school's finished, they're going over.

GRAŻYNA. Well, maybe we can visit him there. But you should find out where it is first.

JASIEK. I think it's in England but I'll check.

GRAŻYNA. You'll love it here, Jasiek. It's a lovely city. I'm in a park right now where there's music playing and tents and people in funny clothes.

JASIEK. And we can fly?

GRAŻYNA. If I work really hard, you can fly.

JASIEK. Cool. Talk to you tomorrow.

GRAŻYNA. Talk to you tomorrow. I love you. Bye.

*She hangs up. The sun is shining. She closes her eyes and enjoys the sun on her.*

Hello, sun.

*JOHN approaches with a tray of samosas.*

JOHN. Samosa?

*GRAŻYNA jumps. Opens her eyes.*

Sorry. I startled you. You were miles away, weren't you?

*GRAŻYNA looks around her and at JOHN, bewildered.*

Nice to finally see some sun, eh?

GRAŻYNA. Yes. Yes.

JOHN. Would you like to try a samosa?

GRAŻYNA. What is this?

*She picks one up.*

JOHN. It's a kind of Indian pastry. Freshly made.

GRAŻYNA. You are Indian?

*She eats a bit of samosa.*

JOHN. Do I look Indian?

GRAŻYNA. No.

JOHN. I'm helping out. There's a festival of Indian culture on. That's what all these tents are. We've got a great bhangra display on later if you're interested. Are you all right?

*GRAŻYNA is coughing and spluttering at the samosa.*

GRAŻYNA. My mouth is fire.

JOHN. Oh dear. Are you not good with spicy food?

GRAŻYNA. Heeeeee – Heeeeeeee –

JOHN. You need a lassi. Come with me.

GRAŻYNA. No.

JOHN. Or some water. Shall I get you some water?

GRAŻYNA *nods*.

## Scene Seven

*12th August 2007*

*Exchange rate: £1 = 5.5744 PLN*

GRAŻYNA *and* PAWEŁ *on the phone*.

GRAŻYNA. You said you were going to arrange it all.

PAWEŁ. I arranged it. I am arranging it.

GRAŻYNA. Have you applied for your passports?

PAWEŁ. Of course I've applied.

GRAŻYNA. When? Because it's the middle of August and –

PAWEŁ. It's all under control, all right? You don't need to do that voice.

GRAŻYNA. What voice?

PAWEŁ. I know what I'm doing. But there's a lot to do. And it's complicated. If we want to do it well, really thoroughly and properly, there's so much you need to do. You can't just arrange it all like that. And this flat business. I've looked into it all and it's really complicated.

GRAŻYNA. What's complicated?

PAWEŁ. All the legal things. And estate agents. I hate estate agents.

GRAŻYNA. Have you spoken to one?

PAWEŁ. One of them came round. What a clown. Total clown. I'm not going to waste my time with him.

GRAŻYNA. Maybe when I'm back, we could go together –

PAWEŁ. I need one I can trust. So I'm going to meet a few more, ask them the right questions, make sure they're not going to rip us off. You need to be so careful.

GRAŻYNA. Do you want me to call some? I can call them from here, if you let me know what questions you need to ask them.

PAWEŁ. And I was thinking. I don't know if it's the right thing for Jaś at the moment. You know what he's like with new things.

GRAŻYNA. I've been looking at flats and schools. I know the area we should move to and there's some nice flats.

PAWEŁ. I think we should wait till Christmas, that'll give me enough time to sort it all out.

GRAŻYNA. Christmas? I might be back by Christmas.

PAWEŁ. Exactly.

GRAŻYNA. But that's five months away.

PAWEŁ. Four.

GRAŻYNA. Almost five.

PAWEŁ. Did Ewa tell you about the internet package?

GRAŻYNA. Internet package?

PAWEŁ. She's got a leaflet about it somewhere. But basically it's phone, internet and TV for 50 złoty a month. 50! That's cheap, isn't it?

*Beat.*

So, what do you think?

GRAŻYNA. About what?

PAWEŁ. About the internet deal.

GRAŻYNA. I think it's good value.

PAWEŁ. So you'll get it?

GRAŻYNA. Me?

PAWEŁ. You know what I mean. Us. You just have to remember the extra 50 złoty every month. But it's hardly anything, is it? What's 50 złoty, that's –

GRAŻYNA. £7. Something like that.

PAWEŁ. £7! That's what you earn in an hour.

GRAŻYNA. Two. After tax.

PAWEŁ. Either way. It's a great deal, isn't it?

GRAŻYNA. Yes.

PAWEŁ. Great.

GRAŻYNA. Paweł –

PAWEŁ. What?

GRAŻYNA. If you come over after Christmas, is it really worth getting this internet package? Won't we just have to cancel it?

PAWEŁ. I don't think so. I don't think it'll be a problem. It's only 50 złoty.

**Scene Eight**

*9th September 2007*

*Exchange rate: £1 = 5.6193 PLN*

GRAŻYNA's *flat in Edinburgh.*

GRAŻYNA. Hello!

LANDLORD. Said you had a problem?

GRAŻYNA. Yes. Please come. Look. Here.

LANDLORD. Right?

GRAŻYNA. Don't you see? There are mushrooms.

LANDLORD. Eh?

GRAŻYNA. Yes, look. Here. This is mushrooms.

LANDLORD. Oh, right enough.

*Beat.*

What do you want?

GRAŻYNA. What do I want? I want that you should – away these mushrooms!

LANDLORD. Just wash it.

GRAŻYNA. Wash it?

LANDLORD. Aye. Bitae bleach and that. That'll get ridae them.

GRAŻYNA. You will wash this carpet?

LANDLORD. No, you wash it.

GRAŻYNA. But this is mushrooms.

LANDLORD. Ah ken what they are. But ahm sayin', wash the carpet, ventilate the place a bit, and you'll no' have them any more. All right?

GRAŻYNA. No, wait. I don't want wash these mushrooms.

LANDLORD. No' ma problem if you cannae be arsed washing yer ain fuckin' hoose.

GRAŻYNA. Sorry?

LANDLORD. I says, it's no' ma problem. Ahv telt ye. Wash the carpet. Bit ae bleach. No problem.

GRAŻYNA. 'No problem'! Yes, problem! No good! This carpet has mushrooms. You cannot clean it. You must take it away and bring new one.

LANDLORD. Look –

GRAŻYNA. Do you understand me? This carpet is dead. Finished. I don't wash it or nothing. You must take it away and bring new one.

LANDLORD. You're talking about removing the whole carpet, for one little patch of mould.

GRAŻYNA. Yes. Whole thing. New one. We want new one.

LANDLORD. That's no' really necessary. What I can do, right, is cut this bit out –

GRAŻYNA. Cut? No.

LANDLORD. Look, it's ma carpet, ma decision, and if ah says ahm gonnae cut it, I'm gonnae cut it.

GRAŻYNA. You can't cut this carpet.

LANDLORD. How no?

GRAŻYNA. Because – because –

LANDLORD. This is my property, right? No' yours. And I've offered to help and you're telling me no, so – I've done what I can, and if you dinnae want ma help, then that's fine wi' me.

*He is on his way out.*

GRAŻYNA. *Poczekaj!* You go?

LANDLORD. What does it look like?

*He exits.*

GRAŻYNA. *Ale nie, nie.* Wait. You must change this carpet. Hey! Mr – Super. *Nie znasz nazwiska.*

Come back here. Come back here and bring me carpet!

**Scene Nine**

*10th September 2007*

*Exchange rate: £1= 5.5788 PLN*

JASIEK *and* GRAŻYNA *on the phone.*

JASIEK. Maybe I can come. Just me.

GRAŻYNA. Darling, I would love you to come, you know that. I miss you very much. All the time. But it's not that easy at the moment.

JASIEK. But when it was all arranged it was easy. You said it was all easy.

GRAŻYNA. It's just more complicated now.

JASIEK. Just cos Dad changed his mind, now I can't come?

GRAŻYNA. You have to come with Daddy.

JASIEK. Why?

GRAŻYNA. I want it to be nice when you come. I want us to have a nice big flat with a big room for you.

JASIEK. Why can't I live where you live now?

GRAŻYNA. Because. Because you can't.

JASIEK. But why not?

GRAŻYNA. Jasiek. Your father and I have decided that you're going to come after Christmas. That's the end of it.

JASIEK. But I want to come now. I've got the money. I saved up.

GRAŻYNA. Really?

JASIEK. From my allowance. Dad gives me it every month but I don't need it all and I save up for my ticket. I made a box. Like a piggy bank. And I've got enough money now, so I could come.

GRAŻYNA. Sweetheart.

JASIEK. You don't want me to come.

GRAŻYNA. I do! I want you to come more than anything. But we're going to do it after Christmas now. You've already started back at school –

JASIEK. Yeah, and I hate it.

GRAŻYNA. And you're going to go to school and study hard and then you'll both come over after Christmas.

JASIEK. I've got all my money saved up.

GRAŻYNA. I know what. Why don't you take some of your money and buy yourself something that you really want? Buy a lovely new toy –

JASIEK. I'm thirteen, Mum, I don't want a *toy*.

GRAŻYNA. Some clothes, then. Buy yourself something nice cos you've been such a good boy, saving up your money.

*Silence.*

Jasiek. Your father and I have decided that you're coming after Christmas. You can't come now. So please stop asking me. Do you hear?

*Silence.*

JASIEK *hangs up.*

GRAŻYNA. Jasiek? Sweetheart?

*She realises he has hung up.*

## Scene Ten

*22nd October 2007*

*Exchange rate: £1 = 5.2425 PLN*

JOHN *and* GRAŻYNA *at Edinburgh Castle.*

GRAŻYNA. It's so beautiful.

JOHN. It used to be the biggest toilet in Scotland.

GRAŻYNA. What?

JOHN. The gardens. What you're looking at. It was a loch. Water. Dark, stinking water. Every house in the Old Town – all of this – threw their toilet buckets and their waste and their dead animals in there.

GRAŻYNA. All this was water?

JOHN. Water… toilets… dead animals… and then they tried witches in it.

GRAŻYNA *doesn't understand.*

You know… hundreds of years ago the people here believed that there were bad women. Possessed by the devil, you know?

GRAŻYNA. 'Devil'? What is 'devil'?

JOHN *points up, then down.*

JOHN. God – and the devil.

GRAŻYNA. Ah, yes.

JOHN. And a witch was a woman who was with the devil. And people blamed them when things went wrong – if your child got sick, or it rained a lot. And to see if they were bad or not, they threw them in the water here. And if you sank – you were innocent. You were with God. And if you floated – you were the devil. And then they killed you anyway. Why are you looking at me like that?

GRAŻYNA. Today is my free day. I want that you show me castle. And you tell me story about toilet and dead women.

JOHN. I'm just being honest with you.

GRAŻYNA. What?

JOHN. I'm just saying what happened. It's all out there. Bones under your feet.

GRAŻYNA. On my free day, I want nice.

JOHN. I know a nice pub near here.

GRAŻYNA. Then we will go there.

**Scene Eleven**

*4th December 2007*

*Exchange rate: £1 = 5.0379 PLN*

EWA *and* GRAŻYNA *on the phone.*

GRAŻYNA. You don't sound very excited.

EWA. Of course I'm excited. Just tell me what day it is so I can put it in my diary.

GRAŻYNA. I haven't bought a ticket yet, but I suppose – if I want to be back on the 23rd, I should probably get the bus on the 21st. So that means I'll be back on the 23rd and we can do the tree and arrange everything and go to mass and visit Gosia and Zbysiek, and Aunty Halinka, and Mariusz and Basia and the twins – my goodness, the twins!

EWA. Can you bring me some books?

GRAŻYNA. Books?

EWA. For uni. There's a couple I absolutely need. *The Business Environment* by Wetherly and Otter.

GRAŻYNA. Hold on, let me write this down. Business what?

EWA. Environment.

GRAŻYNA. How do you spell that?

EWA. Why don't I just e-mail the list to you?

GRAŻYNA. List?

EWA. Look, I have to go. I have a date. I'll e-mail you, okay?

GRAŻYNA. A date?

EWA. He's called Krzysiek.

GRAŻYNA. And what about Jasiek, Ewa –

EWA. I have to go!

GRAŻYNA. What should I get him? Tell me what you think. I want to get him something really nice.

EWA. What's wrong with trainers?

GRAŻYNA. More trainers?

EWA. I tell you what he'd love. He never stops talking about it. Well, it's about the only thing he does talk about. PS2.

GRAŻYNA. What's that?

EWA. Some computer game. It's brilliant, apparently. He needs one or he's going to die.

GRAŻYNA. P-S-2?

EWA. I really have to go.

GRAŻYNA. Is your father there?

EWA. Round at Tadziek's.

GRAŻYNA. Then put Jasiek on.

　　*EWA goes into* JASIEK*'s room.*

EWA. Jasiek? It's Mum, do you want to talk?

　　*EWA covers the phone and mouths.*

It's Mum, are you going to talk to her?

JASIEK *stands still. Does not respond.*

Talk to her.

GRAŻYNA. What's he doing?

EWA. He's doing his homework, Mum, I don't want to interrupt him.

GRAŻYNA. Well – give him a kiss from me and say I'll call again tomorrow.

EWA. All right! Take care, Mum. See you soon. Bye.

*The line goes dead.*

EWA *turns to* JASIEK.

You're a little freak, you know that?

GRAŻYNA *in Edinburgh.*

GRAŻYNA. If a bus leaves Edinburgh bus station at 9 p.m. on Saturday the 21st of December, what time will it arrive in Bydgoszcz? If a woman earns £5.80 an hour and works 8 hours on Monday, Tuesday and Wednesday, then 9.5 hours on Thursday, 8 on Friday and 11.5 on Saturday, how much money does she make? If a woman needs to purchase one copy of *Business Environment* by Wetherly and Otter, priced £32.99, one copy of *Organizational Theory* by Hatch, also priced £32.99, and one copy of *Management Theory and Practice* by Cole, 45 new and used from £19.65, and if she can pack 84 packets of sausages in bacon in one hour, how many sausages does she have to wrap in bacon before she can buy the books? If a Sony PlayStation 2 with console and two games costs £219 – £219? If she loves her son, how much will she spend to show him how much she has missed him over the last 10 months and 19 days? If a bus ticket from Edinburgh to Bydgoszcz costs £59. If the gas bill for the shared residence at 94/8 Girton Mains Road is £217. If overtime is offered to the workers of Halls of Scotland (made in Scotland – by Poles) at the rate of £8.05 an hour. If a woman lives in a stupid country which celebrates Christmas an entire day after it is celebrated in Poland. If a woman lives in a country where no one is even Christian any more. If a woman has to put sausages in trays until the 24th of December to be able to afford the books and the PlayStation and the bus ticket, how can she leave Edinburgh on the 26th of December and arrive in Poland on the 23rd?

PAWEŁ *and* GRAŻYNA *on the phone.*

PAWEŁ. Well, come back on the 28th.

GRAŻYNA. Christmas isn't on the 28th.

PAWEŁ. So we change Christmas.

GRAŻYNA. Christmas is on the 24th.

PAWEŁ. So come back on the 21st.

GRAŻYNA. If I come back on the 21st, I won't have enough money to – for anything.

PAWEŁ. So come back on the 28th.

GRAŻYNA. But I want to be there on the 24th.

PAWEŁ. I'm sure the kids would rather you came later, but with the things they want.

GRAŻYNA (*interrupting*). Well, exactly – what did you say?

PAWEŁ. They'd rather see you a few days later. What difference does it make?

GRAŻYNA. And what about you? What do you want?

JASIEK *enters. He creeps up on his father, holding a rifle to his head.*

PAWEŁ. I don't know. Maybe just some chocolates.

GRAŻYNA. *Organizational Environment*, PlayStation 2 and some chocolates. That's all you want?

PAWEŁ. I think so.

GRAŻYNA. Okay. Fine. I'll – book my ticket. For the 26th.

PAWEŁ. It'll probably be cheaper then too. They always put the prices up for people travelling at Christmas.

JASIEK *shoots his father.*

GRAŻYNA. A cheaper ticket on the 26th. That's what I'll get.

PAWEŁ. It'll be great. Sweetheart?

**Scene Twelve**

*15th December 2007*

*Exchange rate: £1 = 5.0589 PLN*

JOHN *and* GRAŻYNA *on a date.*

GRAŻYNA. I want to do something nice.

JOHN. What do you have in mind?

GRAŻYNA. We will eat haggis.

JOHN. I don't know if that counts.

GRAŻYNA. It's what I want.

JOHN. It's not very Christmassy.

GRAŻYNA. I don't care.

JOHN. All right then. When's your next day off?

GRAŻYNA. No day off.

JOHN. Till when?

GRAŻYNA. 25th.

JOHN. That's illegal.

GRAŻYNA. I have day off from factory. But then I am cleaning.

JOHN. Jesus Christ. Well, when do you want your Christmassy haggis?

GRAŻYNA. Monday or Thursday next week.

JOHN. Then I cordially invite you to the John McIntyre kitchen next Thursday.

GRAŻYNA. Your house?

JOHN. Best haggis in town.

GRAŻYNA. You can cook haggis?

JOHN. Aye, lassie! An' if you're really lucky I'll gie ye a squeeze ae ma tatties an' aw.

GRAŻYNA. No Scottish!

JOHN. Nae Scots, nae haggis.

GRAŻYNA. I don't understand what you are saying me.

JOHN. Then learn.

GRAŻYNA. No.

JOHN. That's very rude.

GRAŻYNA. Why?

JOHN. It's my language.

GRAŻYNA. It's not language. It's 'ew ooo u'.

JOHN. I'll learn your language.

GRAŻYNA. Impossible.

JOHN. Teach me something. Something I can say to you. Nothing rude. Too rude.

GRAŻYNA *thinks for a while.*

GRAŻYNA. *Jesteś cudowną kobietą.*

JOHN. What does that mean?

GRAŻYNA. I don't tell you.

JOHN. Oh-ho. Say it again?

GRAŻYNA. *Jesteś cudowną kobietą.*

JOHN. Yestesh.

GRAŻYNA. *Cudowną kobietą.*

JOHN. Pseudo –

GRAŻYNA. *Cu – dow –*

JOHN. Soo dov –

GRAŻYNA. Cu, cu, nie soo.

JOHN. Tsoo?

GRAŻYNA. *Cudowną.*

JOHN. Soodovna.

GRAŻYNA. *Cu.*

JOHN. Soo.

GRAŻYNA. Cu.

JOHN. Tsoo.

GRAŻYNA. Yes, this one. Cu-dow-na.

JOHN. Tsoo-dov-na.

GRAŻYNA. *Cudowną kobietą.*

JOHN. You're going to kill me.

GRAŻYNA. *Kobietą.*

JOHN. Cob-yet-on.

GRAŻYNA. Ą.

JOHN. O.

GRAŻYNA. Ą. Ą.

JOHN. Ą.

GRAŻYNA. Yes! That it! Say it again! Just like this.

JOHN. Ą.

GRAŻYNA. *Jesteś cudowną kobietą.*

JOHN. I can't. My mouth doesn't work that way.

GRAŻYNA. *Cudowną kobietą.*

JOHN. And what does it mean?

GRAŻYNA. Ha! I don't tell you what it means! You so clever, you can find out yourself.

JOHN. If I say it to the girl in the sandwich shop, will she slap me?

GRAŻYNA. No.

JOHN. I'm going to find out what it means. You wait. Just you wait. By the time you come round for your haggis, I'll have found out.

GRAŻYNA. John. This haggis. At your house. Who will cook it?

JOHN. I will.

GRAŻYNA. And who other people will be there?

JOHN. Other people?

GRAŻYNA. Maybe your family.

JOHN. No family. Just me and you. Yesht tsoo-dov-non-cob-yet-on.

### Scene Thirteen

*24th December 2007*

*Exchange rate: £1 = 4.9585 PLN*

*Music. A beautiful Christmas song.*

JASIEK. It's Christmas time!

EWA. The most wonderful time of the year!

PAWEŁ. And finally you're coming back to us.

ALL. Mummy, our beloved Mummy,
    Our love for you shines like a bright star
    To guide your steps back to our humble home
    Which glow with love for you.

PAWEŁ. I've got the carp!

EWA. A mighty carp!

JASIEK. The biggest carp in Poland!

EWA. Let's set the table –

JASIEK. Let's light the candles –

PAWEŁ. Let's welcome you home.

ALL. Mummy, our beloved Mummy,
    Our love for you shines like a bright star
    To guide your steps back to our humble home
    Which glow with love for you.

JASIEK. We want *kluski*!

EWA. We want *pierogi*!

JASIEK *and* EWA. *Kluski! Pierogi! Kluski! Pierogi!*

PAWEŁ. We know you'll cook it all.

JASIEK. Here's my *opłatek*!

EWA. Here's my *opłatek*!

PAWEŁ. Here's my *opłatek*!

ALL. Mummy, our beloved Mummy,
    Our love for you shines like a bright star
    To guide your steps back to our humble home
    Which glow with love for you.

EWA. A family of joy –

PAWEŁ. A family of peace –

JASIEK. A proper family once again.

ALL. Mummy, our beloved Mummy,
  Our love for you shines like a bright star
  To guide your steps back to our humble home
  Which glow with love for you.

## Scene Fourteen

*28th December 2007*

*Exchange rate: £1 = 4.8786 PLN*

*Bydgoszcz.* JASIEK *plays the following sequence as the others interact around him.*

JASIEK. 'Where's the convoy?' If I don't find my convoy, I'm going to be killed. Check your back, check your front, watch the sides, below me, above me. Nothing, nothing, nothing. Radar dead. Hello? Hello? This is Unit Four, do you read me? Over. Over. Over. Nothing but ocean. Dark ocean. Where's my convoy? How have I lost my convoy? I can't find them! It was a detour! They conned me. What does the commander say? 'Never take your eyes off the controls!' Scan, scan, scan. A blip on the radar. Nothing in the water. Blip blip blip. Can't see anything. A sub. It has to be a sub. Size, speed and depth – it can only be a sub. Enemy or friend? Where's it heading? Where's my convoy? My first duty is to protect the convoy but I have to check out that sub. Friend or foe? Friend or foe? It's the enemy. Two blips. Coming closer. Two subs, two enemy subs, call base, call for back-up, where's my convoy, where are the others, I can't see anything, only black, come on, keep it together, you can do this, focus, do it by feel, engage the torpedoes, engage your torpedoes. Three enemy blips. Louder faster everywhere. Four blips. Torpedoes engaged. I've engaged my torpedoes, if I zigzag, if I dive and surface, dive and surface, it's my only chance. Both torpedoes, straight into the sides. Searing through the water. Like knives. I want there to be an explosion, underwater explosions are beautiful, fire in the water, the men ripped into pieces, metal and limbs tumbling through the water, a hundred points, a thousand points. They're on me! Where did they come from? One two three four! They've fired! No! Fire! Fire! Fire! Torpedoes racing through the dark, traces on my radar, here they come, dive, dive, all I can do is dive. I'm hit. Hit. Hit. Hit. Fire in the water. I'm out, I'm destroyed, my metal, my limbs, tumbling through the water, the black water, nothing but black. I'm out.

GRAŻYNA *enters with a dead carp.*

GRAŻYNA. The carp's dead.

EWA. It's dead?

PAWEŁ. How can the carp be dead? I only bought it –

EWA. Four days ago, Dad. It's been in the bathtub for four days.

GRAŻYNA. And the bathtub is filthy.

EWA. I've been washing at Marta's for the last four days.

GRAŻYNA. The carp is dead, the bathroom is disgusting, there's nothing but eggs and beer in the fridge and Jasiek isn't talking to anyone. What is going on? Who is in charge here?

PAWEŁ. What do you mean?

GRAŻYNA. Here. This. Who's in command? Who wakes up and draws the curtains? Who makes sure the others are up? Who checks when we've run out of milk? Who does the laundry? Who decides what we're going to eat and buys the food and cooks it?

EWA. We all just kind of look after ourselves.

GRAŻYNA. And what about Jasiek? Who checks that he goes to school and comes home and does his homework and doesn't get into fights and brushes his teeth and – plays with his friends?

PAWEŁ. He doesn't really have any friends.

EWA. They all emigrated.

GRAŻYNA. So you've just left him to sit there and play video games?

PAWEŁ. He doesn't want to do anything else.

GRAŻYNA. What has happened to this family?

PAWEŁ. We're fine! We're perfectly fine!

GRAŻYNA. Look at this place. It's a pigsty! We have animals in that factory who live in better conditions than here.

PAWEŁ. You work in a box factory.

GRAŻYNA. No, Paweł, I work in a chilled factory with a saw in one hand and a pig carcass in the other. I work from morning till night and then I do overtime to pay for your clothes and your food and your rent and your internet, phone and TV and I would work there twenty-four hours a day if I could, if I thought it would help make your life better and your life better and my son's life better. Do you hear me? I would work there for the rest of my life if that's what you asked me to do. But in return I expect you to do something for me!

PAWEŁ. Like what?

GRAŻYNA. Clean the fucking house, Paweł! Cook me a fucking meal! Look after our fucking children!

PAWEŁ. Oh that's lovely. Speaking like a common whore now.

GRAŻYNA. Ten months, Paweł, I have spent ten months 'chopping' and 'slicing' and 'removing gristle' and now I come home and you tell me not to talk like a whore?

PAWEŁ. You don't need to swear at us because we haven't got everything organised exactly the way you wanted.

GRAŻYNA. You haven't done anything!

PAWEŁ. We were waiting for you!

GRAŻYNA. What do you want me to do from two thousand miles away? Grow my arms so I can stir your soup and wipe your arses whilst I'm carving pigs up in Scotland?

PAWEŁ. You think it's good enough to just send us money? He's your son, you left him, you think you can just send him money for trainers and everything'll be fine? What about talking to him? What about cuddling him?

GRAŻYNA. Am I the only person who can talk to him? Am I the only person who can cuddle him?

PAWEŁ. You shouldn't have left.

GRAŻYNA. This is all my fault? Well, someone had to go, Paweł, remember? What would we have done? Starved to death whilst we waited for you to find your ID? Have you even done that? Have you? Show it to me! Show me.

PAWEŁ. You've ruined everyone's Christmas, do you know that?

PAWEŁ *starts to walk out*.

GRAŻYNA. Where are you going?

PAWEŁ. To a bar. A nice quiet bar. Thank God it's the 28th and everything is open.

*Exit* PAWEŁ.

GRAŻYNA. Go then. Get out there and work. Take my ticket back to the island. Go and work with dead animals for ten hours a day. Let me stay here with my children. Let me clean my own bath in my own house with my own hands. Let me stay here and be with my family.

EWA. Mum…

It's not normally this bad. It's just – the last few weeks, I don't know, I've been working really hard, and Dad –

I guess we just got confused.

I should have done more, okay? I'm sorry. I wanted everything to be nice for you.

I said sorry.

You know, I'm the only one who works. I'm the only one who studies. I'm the only one who even leaves the flat. What am I meant to do? Come home and cook and clean up after them?

GRAŻYNA. Well, who else is going to do it? Your father can't.

EWA. Yes he can! He's just too lazy. He does nothing. You know that. Nothing. He sits around watching TV until Jasiek comes home and boots him off. He has hands, Mum, he has a brain, maybe a small one but he has a brain, he can turn on a washing machine and boil a pan of pasta exactly the same as I can.

GRAŻYNA. But he's not doing it.

EWA. He's only not doing it cos he thinks someone's going to come home and do it for him, the way they always have. And that's what we're doing now. You send the money home and then I go to Tesco. I go to Tesco, I work an eight-hour shift and then I lug home a crate of economy lager for him. 'You get it, you get the discount, why should I pay 20 złoty for beer when you can get it for 12?'

GRAŻYNA. And your brother? How long has he been like this?

EWA. I don't know. A while.

GRAŻYNA. Weeks? Months?

EWA. It's not like he came into the kitchen and announced it.

GRAŻYNA. Weeks? Months?

EWA. I guess since September. September, October.

GRAŻYNA. Why didn't you tell me?

EWA. I didn't think – I didn't know – I thought he was just, you know, being Jasiek.

GRAŻYNA. Ewa, look at him. He doesn't even know I'm here.

EWA. He does. He's just – he's just playing. When he plays, he doesn't see the world any more. It's just him and the game.

GRAŻYNA. He's sick.

EWA. He's not sick, Mum, he's going to be fine. Now you're here. If you just stay here, Mum, stay here and don't go away again.

GRAŻYNA. Do you really mean that?

EWA. It doesn't work without you, Mum. Can't you see that?

GRAŻYNA. You haven't even finished your first semester, Ewa. Do you really mean that?

EWA *looks away*.

*Silence*.

Well, I'm getting hungry. Is your supermarket still open?

EWA. Every night till ten.

GRAŻYNA. You're going to go shopping. I'm going to write you a list. Whilst you're gone, I'm going to mop and dust and scrub and tidy. Do we have candles?

EWA. We haven't touched them since last year.

GRAŻYNA. I will light some candles, we'll put some straw under the tablecloth – we'll put a tablecloth on the table and we will eat *barszcz* and we will sing songs and we will wish each other a Merry Christmas and we will be a proper family again.

EWA. Are you going to start cooking *barszcz* now?

GRAŻYNA. We're going to cook it together.

EWA. I could get a packet.

GRAŻYNA. Buy beetroot. And onions. We're going to cook it together.

EWA. Okay. There might be *opłatek* on special offer now.

GRAŻYNA. Well, get some.

EWA. Okay.

GRAŻYNA. And if you see your father, tell him he can spend his 28th of December in the bar when he belongs.

## Scene Fifteen

*29th December 2007*

*Exchange rate: £1 = 4.8786 PLN*

GRAŻYNA. Holy Mary, forgive me. Forgive me. Forgive me. I have ruined everything. What must you think of me?

MARIA. Not a lot.

GRAŻYNA. You'll see. I'll make it better. I'm going to stay here and take care of my children and be a good mother.

MARIA. No you're not.

GRAŻYNA. What?

MARIA. I said, no you're not.

*Pause.*

You're going to go back. You're going to go back and take care of your children and be a good mother.

GRAŻYNA. I can't go back!

MARIA. You have to go back! You know that. I know that. What do you want me to say?

*Silence.*

What are you scared of?

GRAŻYNA. Nothing.

*Beat.*

What am I doing? Where am I going?

MARIA. I'm not sure. But isn't that exciting?

GRAŻYNA. No.

MARIA. No? No? You've taken one step, Grażyna, one bite.
And you don't know what else is out there. Do you want to
turn back now?

GRAŻYNA. But is it the right thing?

MARIA. That depends what you want.

GRAŻYNA. I want to be a good mother –

MARIA. No more 'mother'! Forget 'mother'! Forget good!
Forget bad! What do you want?

*Silence.*

You know what I want? I want to chuck you into the ocean.

GRAŻYNA. Holy Mary!

MARIA. I want your lungs to fill with fresh air. I want that little
spark inside you to ignite. I want you to feel alive. Don't you
want that? Look in my eyes and tell me you don't want that.

*Silence.*

See.

GRAŻYNA. Holy Mary, you don't understand.

MARIA. I am the Mother of God, Grażyna, I understand perfectly well.

GRAŻYNA. I am lost, Holy Mary!

MARIA. Lost is good. Lost is interesting. Lost is alive.

GRAŻYNA. I don't know what I'm doing.

MARIA. You're a smart woman, Grażyna. You'll work it out. I
have faith in you.

## Scene Sixteen

*2nd January 2008*

*Exchange rate: £1 = 4.8565 PLN*

GRAŻYNA *with a lump of coal and a bottle of whisky. She rings* JOHN's *doorbell.* JOHN *opens the door.*

JOHN. Well, look who it is. Wonderful woman.

GRAŻYNA. You found out.

JOHN. I found out.

GRAŻYNA. How?

> JOHN *taps his nose.*

> 'Lang may yer lum reek.'

JOHN. Thank you very much. Do you know what it means?

GRAŻYNA. I looked. But I forget. Happy New Year, something like this?

JOHN. You're a bit late.

> GRAŻYNA *checks her watch.*

> It's the second.

GRAŻYNA. First, second, who cares?

JOHN. And you're very late for your haggis.

*Beat.*

GRAŻYNA. I looked on internet. Says I should bring coal and whisky and black bun but I don't know what is black bun.

JOHN. You've got red hair. That's more important than black bun.

GRAŻYNA. Red hair is good?

JOHN. It's very good.

*Beat.*

But not if it stays in the stairwell.

GRAŻYNA. What?

JOHN. If you want to first foot someone, you have to put your foot onto their property. You can't do it from the stairwell.

GRAŻYNA. Can I foot first on second?

JOHN. That's a good question.

GRAŻYNA. It's too late, maybe.

JOHN. You're my first.

GRAŻYNA. Me? Still? First first foot? On second?

JOHN. That's what I said.

GRAŻYNA. No one came yesterday?

JOHN. No.

GRAŻYNA. Oh.

JOHN. So…

GRAŻYNA. I came. For haggis.

JOHN. Did you?

GRAŻYNA. But I couldn't – I wanted to. I thought. I waited. I thought.

JOHN. Then you went home?

GRAŻYNA. Yes.

JOHN. Harder than it looks, eh?

GRAŻYNA. What?

JOHN. The whole foot-over-the-door thing.

GRAŻYNA. It's not hard.

JOHN. You seem to be struggling. And I'm getting cold.

*She crosses over.*

**Scene Seventeen**

*7th January 2008*

*Exchange rate: £1 = 4.8494 PLN*

PAWEŁ *trying to get* JASIEK *to eat.* JASIEK *playing a game.*

PAWEŁ. Guess we should eat something, eh? Are you hungry, son?

She's left us spaghetti. Spaghetti and sauce. To reheat. Do you want some? Are you hungry? Jasiek? You should eat. Jasiek, put that thing down. Are you hungry?

Are you hungry? Shall I heat up this bloody pasta or do you want a pizza?

I know what. Let's do something different. Let's go out. We could go to that place. Near here. The one on top of the video rental place. What's it called? We went there once and you really liked it. 'Crazy Potatoes.' Do you want to go to Crazy Potatoes?

Ach. I'll heat up the pasta.

**Scene Eighteen**

*26th January 2008*

*Exchange rate: £1 = 4.8776 PLN*

EWA *and* GRAŻYNA *on the phone.*

EWA. He went to school! I told you. He went and I cooked spaghetti and he ate it and I'll photocopy his homework and send it to you if you want proof that I'm not lying to you.

GRAŻYNA. Let me talk to him.

EWA *presses the phone against* JASIEK's *ear.*

EWA. Say hi. Just say hi. 'Hi.'

JASIEK *doesn't say anything*.

GRAŻYNA. He has to speak. Make him say something!

EWA. I can't make him talk!

GRAŻYNA. You have to.

EWA. How?

GRAŻYNA. My son, my son.

EWA. Mum, I promise you, we're looking after him.

GRAŻYNA. Put the phone on his ear. If he won't talk to me he has to listen to me.

EWA *puts the phone back up*. JASIEK *wriggles away.*

Darling? It's me, your mummy. Darling, you're going to come over here very soon, do you hear me?

EWA. Jasiek! She's talking to you.

GRAŻYNA. You might have to stay in the same room as me and Kasia when you first get here, but I'm going to earn lots more money so I can get a place for just you and me.

JASIEK *jumps up and runs away.*

EWA. He heard that. He heard everything. He smiled. He's smiling. He's happy, Mum.

GRAŻYNA. You have to tell me the truth.

EWA. I promise you.

GRAŻYNA. Give him a kiss from me. A proper one. Not through the phone.

EWA *kisses* JASIEK.

EWA. From Mum.

GRAŻYNA. Tell him I love him.

EWA *talks to an empty space.*

EWA. Mum says she loves you, Jasiek. And I love you too.

GRAŻYNA. And?

EWA. He's thirteen, Mum. He doesn't like being kissed.

GRAŻYNA. Tell him I'll call him tomorrow. This time.

EWA. She's going to call you again tomorrow. This time. He's nodding.

### Scene Nineteen

*7th February 2008*

*Exchange rate: £1 = 4.8343 PLN*

GRAŻYNA *and* JOHN *on a freezing Scottish beach.*

GRAŻYNA. One year. One year of me. Here.

JOHN. Is this meant to be a celebration?

GRAŻYNA *looks out at the sea.*

I can think of nicer things to do to celebrate. Go inside, for starters.

You're not really celebrating though, are you?

Is everything okay?

*Silence.*

Is this not what you were expecting? Maybe it's not at its best today. But when the sun's shining – I love it here. Most beautiful beach in Scotland.

*Pause.*

Is it this? Are you not happy with this?

GRAŻYNA. What?

JOHN *gestures to them.*

JOHN. This.

GRAŻYNA. No, no.

I just want to see the sea.

*Pause.*

I have a son.

JOHN. Out there?

GRAŻYNA. Coming here.

JOHN. Nice.

GRAŻYNA. You don't understand.

JOHN. No?

GRAŻYNA. Coming here.

JOHN. I understand.

GRAŻYNA. You don't understand.

JOHN. What don't I understand?

GRAŻYNA. If you don't have children, you can't understand.

JOHN. I have two.

GRAŻYNA. What?

JOHN. Jamie is fourteen and Andy is sixteen. Almost seventeen.

GRAŻYNA. You have children?

JOHN. Two.

GRAŻYNA. You never told me.

JOHN. You never told me.

GRAŻYNA. Fourteen and sixteen? Two boys?

JOHN. That's what I said.

GRAŻYNA. Why didn't you tell me?

JOHN. You didn't ask.

GRAŻYNA. You should to tell me.

JOHN. Why should I tell you?

GRAŻYNA. Are they important to you?

JOHN. They're my children.

GRAŻYNA. All this time you have this children and you say nothing?

JOHN. I could say the same thing to you.

GRAŻYNA. Why didn't you tell me?

JOHN. Why should I say something? Do we have to tell each other everything about ourselves?

GRAŻYNA. What else you got that you don't tell me about?

JOHN. Lots of things.

GRAŻYNA. Do you have wife?

JOHN. No. Do you have a husband?

*Silence.*

Okay.

GRAŻYNA. Okay?

JOHN. Was that a yes?

GRAŻYNA. Yes what?

JOHN. Are you married?

*Silence.*

(*Simultaneously.*) I don't mind.

GRAŻYNA (*simultaneously*). I'm married. You don't mind? I say I'm married, you say, 'I don't mind'?

JOHN. What kind of married are you?

GRAŻYNA. 'What kind'?

JOHN. Happily married, unhappily married, don't-really-know married, married-in-name-only, married-cos-you-have-to-be, married-but-soon-to-be-not-married…

GRAŻYNA. I'm just married.

JOHN. Okay.

GRAŻYNA. Okay? I'm married, John.

JOHN. I heard you.

GRAŻYNA. So what?

JOHN. Exactly. So what?

GRAŻYNA. You just going to stand there? 'Okay'?

JOHN. What do you want me to do?

GRAŻYNA. AAAAAAAAAAAAAR-RRRRRRRRRRGGGGGGGGGGG!!!!!!!

*Kurwa* fuck bitch!

JOHN *laughs*.

JOHN. Amazing.

GRAŻYNA. Not amazing! Married.

JOHN. You are amazing and beautiful and sexy.

GRAŻYNA. And married.

JOHN. Okay. Amazing and beautiful and sexy and married.

GRAŻYNA. John. Do something.

JOHN. Like what?

GRAŻYNA. Why are you just stand there? Are you crazy? Do something, say something, Jezus Maria, you should to feel something.

JOHN *lets out a massive bellow*.

JOHN. Like that?

GRAŻYNA. Something like that.

JOHN *picks* GRAŻYNA *up*.

Hey!

JOHN. Scandal!

GRAŻYNA. Put me down. John. Put me down.

JOHN. Into the sea with you. Into the deepest sea. This woman is the devil! Devil, take her!

GRAŻYNA. Stop! Put me down!

JOHN. She is a sinner! Take her!

GRAŻYNA. No! John! Stop! Not into water, John. *Błagam cię, przestań!*

JOHN. One! Two! Three!

**Scene Twenty**

*11th March 2008*

*Exchange rate: £1 = 4.6403 PLN*

JASIEK, EWA and PAWEŁ *go to the passport office*.

PAWEŁ. Right. Come on, son. Let's go.

We have to go today.

If we don't go today –

Come on. Get your jacket, and your shoes.

Jasiek?

Come on. When you've finished this section.

EWA *marches across to* JASIEK *and unplugs him*.

EWA. Move!

JASIEK. Hey!

EWA. We have to go today, Jaś. You can play when we get back.

JASIEK. Can't just unplug me.

EWA. Come on. Jacket. Shoes. Move.

JASIEK *tries to plug himself back in.*

Do you want to go to England to be with Mum?

JASIEK *shrugs.*

Then you need a passport. And Dad needs his new ID. Come on.

JASIEK *moves slowly towards the front door.* EWA *shoots a withering glance at* PAWEŁ.

PAWEŁ. I made sandwiches.

EWA. What?

PAWEŁ. Ham and cheese.

EWA. What do I need a sandwich for?

PAWEŁ. The queues are long.

EWA. You made us all sandwiches? Jasiek, get your shoes on.

PAWEŁ. People are queuing for two or three hours.

EWA. I queued for twenty minutes.

PAWEŁ. You got yours months ago.

EWA. You could have done the same. Jasiek! Shoes!

PAWEŁ. A woman died in Białystok.

EWA. She died?

PAWEŁ. She'd been waiting for three hours.

EWA. Did she die because she was an old *babcia* or did she die because someone clubbed her to death in exasperation?

PAWEŁ. What do I always say? Polish bureaucracy is bad for your health.

EWA. Where's your jacket?

JASIEK. Are we going to die?

EWA. No. We've got sandwiches.

## Scene Twenty-One

*4th April 2008*

*Exchange rate: £1 = 4.4077 PLN*

JOHN *kneels and presents* GRAŻYNA *with a flower. A leaflet folded up like a flower.*

GRAŻYNA. What is this?

JOHN. You said you wanted me to buy you more flowers. Here you go.

GRAŻYNA. This is flower?

JOHN. A-ha. It's a dual-purpose flower. You smell it –

GRAŻYNA. Smells of paper.

JOHN. – 'Oh, how beautiful! Thank you, John! I must cook *bigos* for you like I've been promising to do for the last three months' –

GRAŻYNA. I'm working. Working all the time.

JOHN. – and then you unfold it, and it becomes a beautiful... leaflet on how to deal with uncooperative landlords.

GRAŻYNA. Leaflet?

JOHN. You said you wanted some help.

GRAŻYNA. Yes.

JOHN. So there you go. What does that face mean?

GRAŻYNA. I wanted flowers. Pretty flowers. This is not pretty.

JOHN. But it is very useful.

GRAŻYNA. Useful? A useful leaflet flower?

JOHN. You said you didn't want me to go and speak to him. So this is the next best thing I can do.

GRAŻYNA. Scottish men are crazy.

JOHN. But none of my carpets have mould.

GRAŻYNA. 'It is a landlord's duty to make sure a house meets the Ruzurper Standard.' What the hell is a Ruzurper Standard? '…at the start of the tenancy and at all times during it.' During – *podczas* – *podczas czego*? *Bo. Jeszcze raz.* 'It is a landlord's duty to make sure.' *Jest właściciela* duty to make sure, *czyli robić pewny. Nie.* To make sure: *sprawdzać że wszystko jest poprawnie wykonane.* Okay! Landlord *sprawdza, że* house is *poprawnie wykonane. Dobrze.* Next. 'Ruz – rep – repring. Repairing Standard.' Repairing? *Remont.* If the house meets *remont? Dom spotyka remont?* That doesn't make sense. Why is it meeting? I'm going to call Ewa.

It is the landlord's duto to dum nurger in the billy hoo doo. Will she be at work? 5:15 p.m.? The landlord muss inbiss the house before tiss starts and notting tiss gliss biss diss. I hate this language.

EWA. I've got half an hour, max.

GRAŻYNA. We won't need that long! It's just a few words. Listen. 'The landlord's duty is to make sure a house meets the Repairing Standard.' Repair is *remont*.

EWA. Can you e-mail it to me?

GRAŻYNA. I can't e-mail it to you, I only have a paper one.

EWA. It must be online somewhere.

JOHN. 'Ahm the sheriff round these parts, and if you don't like it, you can git outta town.'

GRAŻYNA. Let me talk to Jasiek first – What are you doing?

JOHN. I'm a sheriff. You know. John Wayne. The necktie. Star badge. Cowboy boots. Sauntering down a dusty road waiting for someone to shoot you.

EWA. Jasiek! It's Mum.

GRAŻYNA. You think this is funny? – Is he there?

JOHN. I'm telling you what a sheriff is.

GRAŻYNA. No, you're laughing at me.

EWA. He's just coming.

JOHN. I'm not.

GRAŻYNA. Just tell me. Please. Who is sheriff here?

JOHN. Oh, here! In Scotland?

GRAŻYNA. Of course in Scotland. Where else?

JOHN. Well, you should have said.

GRAŻYNA. John...

JOHN. The sheriff is like a judge. For less serious cases. Not murder or rape, but things like – parking tickets.

GRAŻYNA. Bad landlord – Hello, sweetiepie! How are you?

JOHN. Exactly.

GRAŻYNA. My house is wind and water. Despite having taken reasonable steps to acquire them, the landlord is willing to carry. If any part of, or anything in, space heating, taking account of the extent to which entitled to use is adversely affected. Sheriff grants and cases landlords in relation to their tenancy, having regard to under the tenancy in reasonable repair.

JASIEK. Gekkos.

EWA. What's that supposed to mean?

GRAŻYNA. That's what you're meant to tell me.

EWA. Mum, I'm meant to be going to Marta's…

GRAŻYNA. I have spent the last twelve months working in a pig factory to pay for your education, Ewa – What's 'gekkos'?

EWA. Let me get my dictionary.

GRAŻYNA. And what is 'sheriff grants'?

JOHN. What?

GRAŻYNA. 'There are sheriff grants.' This is money, right?

JASIEK. They're everywhere. They guard the warehouses.

EWA. 'Grant' *to stipendium*.

GRAŻYNA. *Stipendium?*

EWA. Maybe the sheriff gives grants to people to fix their homes.

JOHN. Sheriffs don't give grants.

JASIEK. You got to kill them but so they don't notice.

GRAŻYNA. It says here they do.

JOHN. Let me see that. No, Grażyna, they grant consent. Look – 'a sheriff grants consent' – as in, he says 'yes'.

GRAŻYNA. And wind and water?

JOHN. Wind and water *tight*, woman. The property has to be wind and water tight.

GRAŻYNA. 'Wind tight'? My house has to be tight? How can I make it tight? – You shouldn't kill things, Jasiek, that's not nice.

JOHN. Tie it up. Really firmly.

GRAŻYNA. Tie it up?

JOHN. With rope. Or cling film. Cling film's my favourite.

GRAŻYNA. I kill you! I tie you up in cling film.

JOHN. Really?

EWA. Do you want to talk to Dad?

GRAŻYNA. Fixture. 'Something securely, and usually permanently' – *Boże, nie mogę!*

EWA (*reading from dictionary*). 'A permanently fixed item in a house, such as a bath, which would not be taken by someone when they move to a new home: "all fixtures and fittings are included in the price." *Figurative*: They've been at it so long he's become a permanent fixture in her life.'

GRAŻYNA. What's that supposed to mean?

EWA. That's what it says.

JASIEK. Sometimes there's just two or three of them.

GRAŻYNA. Is a carpet a fixture? It is not permanently fixed. You might take it.

EWA. Like a bath. Or a cupboard.

GRAŻYNA. Fitting… Fit – correct size. Fit – position. Fit – suit. Does your suit fit? Does the fit suit you? I am fit. I am suit. It doesn't suit me. It doesn't fit me.

EWA. Mum! Concentrate.

JASIEK. You can just slit their throats.

GRAŻYNA. It's a ridiculous language – 'Any baths, fittings – ' Now – is a carpet a fitting?

EWA. How am I meant to know if a 'carpet' is a 'fitting'?

GRAŻYNA. I don't like the sound of that at all – Baths, maybe carpets and appli…

EWA. 'Appliances' *to AGD.*

GRAŻYNA. Really? That's an appliance? A fridge is an appliance? Why don't they just say?

JASIEK. In the weapons depot there's like twenty of them. Maybe thirty. They always get me. They just come at you like RAAAAAAA.

EWA. '…are in reasonable repair and proper working order.'

GRAŻYNA. Does a carpet have reasonable repair? What is its proper working order? – And what about school? How's school?

JOHN. What do you want from a carpet?

GRAŻYNA. What do I want from a carpet?

JOHN. How should it be?

JASIEK. I've got to crack the weapons depot.

GRAŻYNA. Shouldn't be anything! Should just be there!

JOHN. It should be clean.

GRAŻYNA. Yes. Clean, of course. No holes. At the edges, should be nice, not all… (*She mimes fibres coming undone.*) And are you saving money for your ticket?

JOHN. Frayed.

GRAŻYNA. Afraid?

EWA. '*Jeśli komitet uzna, że właściel dopuścił się zaniedbania obowiązków…*' Mum…

JASIEK. I've tried everything I can think of and I can't do it. They kill me every time.

GRAŻYNA. So 'reasonable repair' means 'no mushrooms'.

JOHN. I would say so.

EWA. Mum, look on the website…

JASIEK. The first two are easy. One, two, three. Then you can shoot the next one, use him as a shield for the crossfire, and shelter next to the truck.

GRAŻYNA. This leaflet say that carpets cannot have mushrooms, or landlord will be punished by sheriff.

JOHN. Exactly.

GRAŻYNA. Hah! 'If your carpet has mushrooms, your landlord must make it nice.' – And you know, Jasiek, I spoke to Bartek's mum in Limerick and we're definitely going to visit them once you've come over.

JOHN. '...must make sure the house meets the Repairing Standard.'

EWA. Mum?

GRAŻYNA. 'Repairing standard' is anti-mushroom law.

JOHN. 'Here in the Wild West, we don't like men who let their fixtures get into disrepair.'

GRAŻYNA. Ha!

JASIEK. Bartek?

EWA. Mum. There's a Polish translation on the website.

GRAŻYNA. What?

EWA. '*Co to jest należyty stan użytkowo-techniczny* (repairing standard?)'

GRAŻYNA. Let me see that.

EWA. '*Wymogi te są bardzo podstawowe. Lokal zgodny jest ze standardem użytkowym, jeśli...*'

GRAŻYNA. '*...jest zabezpieczony przed wiatrem i wodą i nadaje się do zamieszkania.*' I don't believe it! In Polish! Where did you find this?

EWA. Top-left corner.

GRAŻYNA. '*Konstrukcja i zewnętrzny stan budynku (w tym rynny, ścieki i zewnętrzne rury) są w dobrym stanie i sprawnie działają.*'

JOHN. Please stop.

EWA. '*Meble, wyposażenie i urządzenie oddane w użytkowanie lokatorom są...*

EWA *and* GRAŻYNA. *... są w dobrym stanie i sprawnie działają!*'

JOHN. What the hell does that mean?

GRAŻYNA. It means Jasiek is coming to stay with me.

## Scene Twenty-Two

*17th May 2008*

*Exchange rate: £1 = 4.2466 PLN*

GRAŻYNA'*s flat.*

LANDLORD. Some people would be quite happy wi' that carpet.

GRAŻYNA. We are not happy.

LANDLORD. 'We'?

GRAŻYNA. Everyone who lives here. The tenants.

LANDLORD. All fuckin' thirteen of you?

GRAŻYNA. There are five tenants at this property. Me, Mrs Kasia Tuszynska, Mr Grzegorz Gasiorek, Mr Piotr Krzyżanowski and Mr Tomasz Lewandowski.

LANDLORD. Fuckin' delighted for ye. Let's have a party.

GRAŻYNA. With Mr Tomasz Lewandowski, you signed tenancy agreement.

LANDLORD. Course I did.

GRAŻYNA. I have it here. You see. 'Signed, tenant: Tomasz Lewandowski; signed, landlord: Mr Brian Hunter.' That is you, Mr Brian Hunter, yes?

LANDLORD. Last time I looked.

GRAŻYNA. In this tenancy agreement is listed 'carpet', as part of inventory. Here.

LANDLORD. Right, there's no need to wave that thing in ma face, all right? I can fuckin' hear ye, ahm no' deaf. Get it oot ma face!

GRAŻYNA. Mr Hunter. I would like you please to replace this carpet. According to the agreement in our tenancy contract.

LANDLORD. Ahm no' replacin' anything.

GRAŻYNA. You must replace this carpet. It is your responsibility.

LANDLORD. Dinnae fuckin' talk to me about responsibilities. I ken what ma responsibilities are, and they dinnae fuckin' include that thing!

GRAŻYNA. I think they do.

LANDLORD. You made it like that. You sort it out.

GRAŻYNA. No. We did not make this, and we will not sort it out. You will sort it out.

LANDLORD. Oh, so now you're telling me what to do? That's not how it fuckin' works. I say what I will and willnae do for ye, and if you dinnae like it, you can fuck off. Hear me? Get your things and fuck off.

GRAŻYNA. You want me to leave?

LANDLORD. If you're going to be an awkward fucking bitch, then aye. That's exactly what I want.

GRAŻYNA. You can't do that.

LANDLORD. Yes I fuckin' can. Rent arrears, damage to the property, I can evict you any time I like. The whole fuckin' lot of ye, if I have to.

GRAŻYNA. Mr Hunter, I am simply ask you to replace a carpet which is mushrooms. I mean mouldy. There is no problem, you don't have to get angry, please...

LANDLORD. Get off ma fuckin' property.

GRAŻYNA. You can't do this!

LANDLORD. Ahv had enough of this shite, I really have.

GRAŻYNA. Mr Hunter. You will not replace this carpet?

LANDLORD. No I fuckin' won't!

GRAŻYNA. Then I will take you to PRHP!

LANDLORD. To what?

GRAŻYNA. Private Rented Housing Panel. You have a duty to repair and we have tenancy agreement and I am asking you to take away this mouldy carpet because it is a risk to our health. Will you do that?

LANDLORD. No!

GRAŻYNA. Then I will take you to the panel.

LANDLORD. And what are they going to do about it?

GRAŻYNA. First, we will try mediation. Then, if you still refuse, they will make enforcement order. And if you still refuse, they will impose rent-relief order.

LANDLORD. For fuck's sake.

GRAŻYNA. Do you want that?

LANDLORD. What is it? The PHR-what?

GRAŻYNA. PRHP. Here is a leaflet, with all informations.

LANDLORD. Jesus Christ.

GRAŻYNA. Mr Hunter. This is just a carpet. I am not asking you to install swimming pool or put on new roof or turn everything to gold. I am simply asking you to replace a mouldy carpet. Will you do that, or do I need to phone my friends at PRHP?

LANDLORD. All right, all right, I'll fix the fucking carpet. Jesus Christ.

GRAŻYNA. When?

LANDLORD. When I get a new one!

GRAŻYNA. We would like it this week. Please.

LANDLORD. Gonnae tell me what fuckin' colour you want an' all?

GRAŻYNA. Blue.

LANDLORD. Blue. A blue carpet.

GRAŻYNA. Yes. A beautiful blue new carpet. A carpet that you can feel under your feet and say 'mmm'. A carpet that makes me feel like a normal human being, in my house, and not like an animal who lives in the forest. Just a normal carpet. A carpet my son can walk on and not feel ashamed that his mummy is living in a house of mushrooms.

Do you understand?

LANDLORD. I understand.

GRAŻYNA. And you will do this for me?

LANDLORD. I said yes!

GRAŻYNA. YES!

*She has a moment of celebrating her triumph.*

Yes, you will change this for me. Yes, you will listen to me. Yes, you will make it exactly how it should be.

You know, there are several other changes I would like to make to this flat. Here, I would like the floor not to squeak. Here, I would like the cupboard door to close properly. Here, I would like the wind to stay outside. Here, I would like not to hear the neighbours play techno very early in the morning and very late at night. Here, I would like the food to taste the same way it tastes at home. Here, I would like my family to be sitting and eating *obiad* all together. Here, I close the door and I am totally alone. No one come to ask me for anything, no one come to talk to me, no one want anything from me. This, I love. This, I don't want to change.

*The phone rings.*

Hello? Oh. Hi.

But I want you to do it.

Yes, but I want you to do it.

Children fly alone all the time. You'll be with him in Warsaw and I'll be waiting at this end and nothing can go wrong.

He's fourteen, he's not a baby, he'll be absolutely fine. Will you book his ticket? Paweł?

Thank you.

*She hangs up.*

*An idea hits her.*

'Do you have mouldy carpet?

Do you have uncooperative landlord?

I can help you.

Call Grażyna on 07784 567 345.'

EWA *on the phone to* GRAŻYNA.

EWA. What do you mean, 'set up a business'?

GRAŻYNA. A business. My own business. To earn some more money.

EWA. You?

GRAŻYNA. Me.

EWA. But what are you going to sell?

GRAŻYNA. Knowledge.

EWA. You can't sell knowledge.

GRAŻYNA. I know how landlords function. I know the language. I know the law.

EWA. Who's going to pay for that?

GRAŻYNA. There are forty thousand Poles in Edinburgh. And not all of them have university educations.

EWA. How much are you going to charge them?

GRAŻYNA. I don't know – £10?

EWA. Have you even done any market research? You can't set up a business, Mum, you don't have a clue.

*A phone call.*

KRZYSZTOF. I saw your advert. Can you help me? It's about box 14A. Do I put in the tax-deducted figure, or the pre-tax figure?

GRAŻYNA. I don't do tax –

EWA. Never say 'no'! You speak the language, you know the law – figure it out.

GRAŻYNA. Not tax law!

EWA. He is potential income. Never say 'no' to potential income.

GRAŻYNA. Box 14A. Let me have a look. In box 14A you must enter the figure of the sum that you entered in box 9G, minus any deductions. What's a deduction?

EWA. 'Problems filling in your tax return? Call tax expert Grażyna on 07784 567 345.'

*A phone call.*

BARTEK. But if I was self-employed in box 12, and employed in subsheet 76B, what do I put in box 32E?

GRAŻYNA. Box 32E is simply the sum you entered in box 14, plus the sum you entered in box 14E, and if you have any further declarations to make on the self-employed sheets, you should do that here.

KRZYSZTOF. Thank you very much! That's made it all clear!

BARTEK. £14,349. £210.98. £13,964? You're sure? Thank you very much!

*A phone call.*

JOLA. I saw your advert online. It's not about my tax return, but I thought you might be able to help.

GRAŻYNA. One per cent for tax returns.

EWA. See if you can get away with two. And you should have a minimum charge.

JOLA. I have water pouring through my ceiling. I've been up to the neighbours upstairs, but they're not answering and it's pouring through the light and down the walls like a waterfall.

GRAŻYNA. Hello? Council water department? I am calling on behalf of my friend Mrs Jolanta Wojtkiewicz. She has water pouring through her ceiling. 34/5 Lower Briar Avenue. W-O-J-T-K-I-E-W-I-C-Z. No. W-O-J-T-K-I-E- No. K-I-E –

*A phone call.*

BARTEK. Mrs Grażyna, it's me again. I just wanted to check with you. Where do I put the holiday pay?

GRAŻYNA. Spell it how you want. Are you going to send someone round or not?

SUPERVISOR. Grażyna! Your last break was twenty minutes long. Get off that phone and get back to work.

GRAŻYNA. Very sorry. It's my family, my son, he's sick.

SUPERVISOR. I've got my eye on you.

*A phone call.*

ASIA. We want to register our child for school. How do we do that?

GRZESIEK. And he's sick. We need to take him to the doctor. Can you make an appointment for us?

GRAŻYNA. If you can't pay, I'm afraid I can't help you.

EWA. £100 in a week? You're joking?

GRAŻYNA. Before tax.

EWA. Really?

GRAŻYNA. Really.

EWA. You did that? By yourself?

GRAŻYNA. Of course by myself! Who else is going to help me?

EWA. I'm – I'm – I don't know what to say.

GRAŻYNA. Well that's a first too.

EWA. Ha ha ha.

GRAŻYNA. Next week, £200.

EWA. I wish I was there! I want to see this with my own eyes.

GRAŻYNA. You're going to come over after your exams, aren't you?

EWA. Absolutely. You can be my marketing case study for next year.

GRAŻYNA. Can I speak to Jasiek?

EWA. He's out.

GRAŻYNA. Where?

EWA. He and Dad went out to some horrible restaurant. The one above the video rental place.

GRAŻYNA. Crazy Potatoes?

EWA. That's the one. Krzysiek's taking me out for sushi.

GRAŻYNA. And he's happy?

EWA. He loves sushi.

GRAŻYNA. *Jasiek.*

EWA. Oh.

GRAŻYNA. Is he excited about coming?

EWA. Call his mobile, Mum, tell him about the business.

GRAŻYNA. This restaurant – it's just him and your father there?

EWA. I think so.

GRAŻYNA. I'll text him. He can call me when they're finished.

EWA. I'm so proud of you.

GRAŻYNA. You're proud of me?

### Scene Twenty-Three

*27th May 2008*

*Exchange rate: £1 = 4.3034 PLN*

PAWEŁ *and three* JASIEKS *at the airport.*

JASIEK 1. What do you think?

JASIEK 3. I don't like it. You?

JASIEK 1. I don't know. You?

JASIEK 2. Blood's pumping in my veins.

PAWEŁ. You've got your passport?

JASIEK 1. Metal detectors, guards, controls, lanes.

JASIEK 3. People, people, people, people.

JASIEK 2. Let's scale the roof.

JASIEK 1. Let's just wait here.

PAWEŁ. And you've got your boarding card. Hold on to them, you hear me?

JASIEK 2. The roof is the only way.

JASIEK 3. Are you crazy? There could be anything on the roof. Infrared lasers, tracers, dogs.

JASIEK 1. We just have to get to the plane.

PAWEŁ. Guess that's all.

JASIEK 3. I don't like the mission! I don't like it! I'm not going!

JASIEK 2. We're a team! A unit! We stick together.

JASIEK 3. They will execute us, do you understand? We don't know what's out there and you want us to hand over everything we have and just walk? We don't know what's out there, we have no weapons, we don't know what's there and you're saying 'walk'? We will die. Do you hear me? We will die.

PAWEŁ. Just got to wait for this lady from the plane.

JASIEK 2. Death. Fire. Petrol. Dogs. Chains. Guns.

JASIEK 3. A storm. The apocalypse.

PAWEŁ. And you've got your sandwich?

JASIEK 1. We just need to get to the plane.

JASIEK 3. And then? And then? And then? Get to the plane, and then what?

JASIEK 2. Get to the plane or die trying.

JASIEK 1. Are you going to come?

JASIEK 3. Is he going to come?

PAWEŁ. It's difficult.

JASIEK 1. He won't come.

JASIEK 3. She doesn't want him. He can't come.

JASIEK 2. We don't need him! What is he, and he's nothing, he's useless, we don't need him. Cut him off. Let him go. Let him drown.

JASIEK 1. You've got your ID. You can come any time.

JASIEK 3. It's not about the ID! You know that!

JASIEK 2. He's a useless sack of shit and we don't need him.

PAWEŁ. You go out there first. You be with your mum and then we'll see where we're at.

JASIEK 1. He could help us.

JASIEK 2. How?

JASIEK 1. One day. Somewhere. Something.

JASIEK 3. He won't come. Look at him. He'll never come.

PAWEŁ. Everything's going to be fine, son. Everything's going to be fine.

JASIEK 2 (*to* PAWEŁ). I hate you. I hate you. I hate you.

JASIEK 1 (*to someone else*). I hate you. I hate you. I hate you.

JASIEK 3. Who are we? What are we doing? Where are we going?

PAWEŁ. Call me as soon as you land.

JASIEK 3. Dad!

JASIEK 1. Let go of him! You coward! You child! You pathetic wretched snivelling dog.

JASIEK 2. Get up! Get up and fight! You're a man, a soldier, get up and fucking fight.

JASIEK 3. Let go of me!

PAWEŁ. You're going to be flying! Just think about that, how great it'll be to fly.

JASIEK 1. We move as one. We are one. Let him go.

JASIEK 2. Together?

JASIEK 3. Together.

JASIEK 1. Together. Let's move.

JASIEK 3. Goodbye.

JASIEK 1. Goodbye.

JASIEK 2. I hope you fuckin' die.

JASIEK 3. And you'll come? And you'll call? And we'll chat? You remember how to chat, like I showed you, you log in, you can see if I'm online with the icon, and we can chat, and you have to press return, you remember?

JASIEK 2. Come on! Movin' out! Boots on our feet and blood in our veins.

JASIEK 1. We just need to get to the plane.

JASIEK 3. And then?

PAWEŁ. Bye! Bye! Have a good trip. Bye!

JASIEK 2. And then. Tomorrow. Next level. Next game. Walk, fight, learn.

JASIEK 1. We'll get it. We'll crack it, we'll destroy anyone in our path.

JASIEK 2. We're leaving you here, you understand? Cos you're nothing to us. Never were, never will be.

JASIEK 3. You will come, won't you?

JASIEK 2. Come on! Come on! Come on!

MARIA. Hello, Jasiek. I'm Maria. I'm going to be looking after you on the flight. Shall we go?

JASIEK 3. Nice tits.

JASIEK 1. Nice arse.

JASIEK 2. Let's fucking shoot her.

MARIA. If you move so much as a finger without my permission I will see to it that you never arrive anywhere, do you hear me?

JASIEK 1. Fuck.

JASIEK 3. Fuck.

JASIEK 2. Fuck!

JASIEK 1. Who are you?

MARIA. I'm Maria. And I'm watching you. Shall we go?

## Scene Twenty-Four

1. If a woman waits

3. If a woman loves

1. If a woman is in love

4. If a woman is loved

1. If a woman fears

2. If a woman hopes

1. If there is an ocean

3. If there is a woman

2. If a woman is separated by an ocean

4. If a child is above the ocean

1. Not here nor there

3. And here and there

1. If we are waiting

2. If we are searching

1. If we are always moving

4. If we are here and there

3. If we are always and never

2. If here is there

1. If I am here

2. If I am here

1. If I am here

3. If you are here

4. If I am there

2. If I do not know where you are

1. If I do not know where I am

3. If I will always be here

4. If I can never know

2. If you are always somewhere else

1. If love is not

3. If love is neither here nor there

4. Nor here

2. But here

1. And there

3. If money is here

2. But I am there

1. If love is money

4. If love is always

3. If the distance is too far

1. If my arms cannot stretch

2. If my heart has broken

3. If my faith has gone

4. If you take her hope

1. If he gives me hope

2. If you could draw a line

3. If you were a boundary

4. If I were hope

1. If you were me

> JASIEK *comes out of the arrivals hall.* GRAŻYNA *is waiting.*

JASIEK. Hi.

> *The End.*

APPENDICES

## A Rough Guide to Polish Pronunciation

POLISH    ENGLISH

Ż         Like 'j' in the French words 'je' or 'journal'
Ł         W
W         V
J         Y
CZ        CH
SZ        SH
SI        Similar to 'sh' but softer
ZI        Similar to 'je' but softer
Y         Similar to 'uh' in English, not 'eee' or 'i'

Stress is always on the penultimate syllable.


Grażyna – Gra-je-nah

Paweł – Pav-vew

Ewa – Ev-va (as in 'never ever')

Jasiek – Yash-ek

John – Dżon


Antkiewicz – Ant-k-yeah-vitch

Bydgoszcz – Byd-goshch

Wyższa Szkoła – Vyj-shah Shko-wah

Robert Dziekanski – Robert Dje-kan-ski

## Polish Translations

### Scene Three

| | |
|---|---|
| *Biały* | White |
| *Wszystko biały* | Everything [is] white |
| *Noc* | Night |
| *Nie* | No |

### Scene Four

The workers in this scene speak their own special version of Polish, and the words they attempt to say in Polish are written phonetically to reflect this. So for example, the line '*imye, nazwisko, adres, prasa*' is the equivalent of '*imię, nazwisko, adres, praca*' in correct Polish (meaning 'first name, surname, address, work').

| WORKERS' VERSION | CORRECT POLISH | ENGLISH |
|---|---|---|
| Dobshe? | *Dobrze?* | Good; 'all right, got it?' |
| Too tie pod pea satch | *Tutaj podpisać* | Sign here |
| Spontachka | *Sprzątaczka* | Cleaning lady |
| Fabrica | *Fabryka* | Factory |

GRAŻYNA.

| | |
|---|---|
| *Fabryka? W fabryce? Jest praca?* | Factory? In a factory? Is there work? |

### Scene Five

GRAŻYNA.

| | |
|---|---|
| *Poczekaj!* | Wait! |
| *Ja…* | I… |
| *Ale gdzie?* | But where? |
| *Proszę pana!* | Excuse me! [To a man.] |

| | |
|---|---|
| *Głowa* | Head |
| *Ale co mam zrobić z głową?* | But what am I meant to do with the head? |
| *Niech ktoś mi powie co mam zrobić!* | I want someone to tell me what I have to do! |
| *Czterdzieści dwa funty* | Forty-two pounds |

## Scene Eight

GRAŻYNA.

| | |
|---|---|
| *Ale nie, nie* | But no, no |
| *Super* | Super, great |
| *Nie znasz nazwiska* | You don't know his name |

## Scene Nineteen

GRAŻYNA.

| | |
|---|---|
| *Kurwa!* | Fuck! |
| *Błagam cię, przestań!* | I'm begging you, stop it! |

## Scene Twenty-One

GRAŻYNA.

| | |
|---|---|
| *Podczas* | During |
| *Podczas czego?* | During what? |
| *Jeszcze raz* | One more time |
| *Jest właściciela 'duty'* | It is the landlord's duty |
| *Czyli robić pewny* | literal but meaningless translation of 'to make sure' |
| *Sprawdzać, że wyszystko jest poprawnie wykonane* | to make sure that everything has been done properly |
| *Dom spotyka remont?* | literal but meaningless translation of 'house meets repairs' |
| *Boże, nie mogę!* | God, I can't do this! |

EWA.

| | |
|---|---|
| *'Grant' to stipendium* | 'Grant' is grant |
| *'Appliances' to AGD* | 'Applicances' are appliances |

Ewa and Grażyna then quote from the Polish translation of the leaflet:

| | |
|---|---|
| *Jeśli komitet uzna, że właściel dopuścił się zaniedbania obowiązków…* | If the committee decides that the landlord has neglected his responsibilities… |
| *Co to jest należyty stan użytkowo-techniczny (repairing standard?)* | What is the Repairing Standard? |
| *Wymogi te są bardzo podstawowe. Lokal zgodny jest ze standardem użytkowym, jeśli…* | The requirements are very straightforward. A property meets the Repairing Standard if… |
| *…jest zabezpieczony przed wiatrem i wodą i nadaje się do zamieszkania* | …it is wind and water tight and fit for habitation |
| *Konstrukcja i zewnętrzny stan budynku (w tym rynny, ścieki i zewnętrzne rury) są w dobrym stanie i sprawnie działają* | The structure and exterior of the property (including drains, gutters and external pipes) are in reasonable repair and proper working order |
| *Meble, wyposażenie i urządzenie oddane w użytkowanie lokatorom są… w dobrym stanie i sprawnie działają* | Fixtures, fittings and appliances provided under the tenancy are in reasonable repair and proper working order |

**Things People Said to Us**

*As part of the research into Cherry Blossom, the creative team
(LC, CG, LW and MG) spoke to a wide range of people in
Scotland and Poland, from factory workers to academics. The
following has been taken from those conversations:*

* I'm really surprised, actually, that you're doing this project.
I'm surprised that people would be interested in Poland. * How
can you say yes to Poles and no to Bulgarians? * A man asked
me, where are you from, and I said Poland. And he didn't know
where is Poland! And I said, you know, near Germany, he didn't
know either. * The change is not that this generation is
emigrating, it's that they are the first ones who might go back. *
I came here in 2004, before we had joined the EU. So I needed
a work permit. I got job in this Turkish coffee shop, it was one
of only places where they did not want to see work permit. It
was right opposite police station, but police don't care if you are
illegal because that is Home Office. But it was nice, then. Not
everyone was saying to you, oh, you are so many Polish… and
then May 1st came and in one day there were already so many
people and in one week, it changed totally. * Sometimes I think
people coming here do expect that they're going to get off the
bus and there'll be a big sign up: 'rooms', and another one
saying 'work'. And of course it's not like that. * Don't talk to
me about Bydgoszcz! I'm the wrong man! You know there's
this rivalry between my hometown Toruń and Bydgoszcz. Toruń
is really beautiful. That's where the astronomer Copernicus was
born. Bydgoszcz… there's nothing there. * We're in the
spotlight here. * There was a time in Ireland where you had to
know a politician, a teacher and a priest to get a job in the
council. The wheeling and dealing in Ireland and the corruption,
it's very similar to Poland. * We could not be equal to the
British in Britain, but we could hold moral superiority, we are a
pure nation. * It's pro-rata, the number of Poles involved in

crime is about right, I mean for the number of them here it's
pretty much spot on, the same number of crimes and criminals
as you'd get with the same number of Scots. * Poland is the
Christ of Europe. * The Scottish church is very joyful. * We call
Bathgate Baghdad. It's easier to pronounce. * I always say, I
was unlucky in that I was born in Poland. Unlucky. It's my
home, and I hope that I can spend my last days in the place
where I have my roots. But I don't know when that'll be, fifteen
years, twenty years, eight months... * This guy was getting
drunk on the plane and not cooperating and the stewardess was
asking if anyone spoke Polish and I was quiet, I didn't want to
be associated with him, people to think of me and some peasant
drinking vodka and eating boiled eggs. * You see it if you look
at the application procedure to work at the council. They're
looking at all these application forms and they see the Polish
name, and they think, oh, he won't speak good English. Poles
are good workers, but only for Kettle's. And it's frustrating, cos
they're not looking at the CVs, at the skills, and there are
skilled workers in unskilled jobs. And you look at the council
and it's like, well, how did you get where you are? Cos some of
the people there... * Trade moves the same way as war. This is
only one of Poland's problems. * I am human being, Gestaltist
Buddhist Pole. * In Donegal in the '80s, whole villages
emigrated to the USA. There was a hopelessness with the
political situation, the corruption, there was no hope. And they
were emigrating to Chicago and working on building sites there
and earning more than they ever could have in Ireland. And
then they began to see the value of the dollar fall, and realised
that they could earn more on a building site back home than in
Chicago. * Capitalism is not good for spirituality. Money is not
an ally of ideas. * You get what I call emigration syndrome,
where you start idealising your home, you know, the people
from your home, or you start reading poetry that you would not
have read before. * Some at the magazine say we should stop
writing about bad things, because this will only encourage
people to go back to Poland, we should write about happy,
successful Poles. * *Polak Polakowi wilkiem jest*. [A Pole is a
wolf to other Poles.] * You can live on £1 a day because you

can buy economy beans for 16p, bread for 17p. Rice pudding as a Sunday treat. That's 5 złoty. And there's no way you could live on 5 złoty a day in Poland. * I ask them, what are you proud of, and they don't know what to say. They say they're not proud of anything, of being Polish, they would like to forget that they're Polish. I would like them to understand that they don't have to feel worse, that they can be proud to be Polish, you don't have to feel worse just cos you are Polish. * We moved from one certainty to another certainty. * It took me a while to learn how to work as little as my Scottish colleagues. * The better you are networked, the better you are resourced. * Poles abroad work harder than Poles in Poland. * I always feel very at home in Ireland. * We don't want to talk about Communism! * What we have to do is decide what to do with the time given to us. * In Western Europe, there's a strong attachment to the law. People think, in general, that it would be better for society if everyone obeyed the law. In Eastern Europe, laws exist to be broken. Because there is no good reason to keep them. People think they are cleverer than the law-makers. So a British person would always keep their mobile turned off in a plane, for example, but Poles would turn them on as soon as they land because they know there's a law about this, and it's wrong. * I don't know anyone who's emigrated. Nobody. * *Nie wybaczę ci, Polsko.* [I can't forgive you, Poland.] * Literature spoke to people in the nineteenth century. But not this generation, they don't read. The language isn't evolving, it's going back. * They're not emigrants. An emigrant comes for good. They're tourists. * In Eastern society, close friends want to be as close as possible. In the West, we protect our private sphere. * Everyone kept saying, oh, it's so nice that you're in Europe now. And I was like, I thought we always were European. * Everything is Polish – Drambuie is Krupnik. * I am sure, I hope, I will go back. * You wait and see – as soon as it hits 4 złoty to the pound they'll all go home, ideology is nothing, it's all economics.

**The Reported Chronology of Robert Dziekanski
at Toronto Airport**

*The following took place between 15:12 on the 14th October
2007 and 02:20 on the 15th October 2007.*

At 15:12, Robert Dziekanski (43) arrives at Vancouver
International Airport on Condor Airlines Flight DE6070 from
Frankfurt. Earlier that day he had left Poland on his first ever
flight.

His mother, Zofia Cisowski, and her husband are waiting for
him beyond immigration at the meet-and-greet area.

Between 15:35 and 16:09, it is known that he enters the customs
hall along with 80–100 other passengers. All other passengers
line up for primary inspection and in turn clear the area.

Once all of the other passengers have moved through the
customs hall, Robert approaches one of two customer-service
agents and stands, staring directly into the man's eyes. He then
wanders to a table where there are instructions for completing
customs declaration forms. Another customer-service agent
approaches Mr Dziekanski and asks if he has a form. Mr
Dziekanski does not respond. He is reported to have been pale,
sweating profusely and staring at the ground.

As Mr Dziekanski speaks no English, the customer services
agent gestures him towards a customs officer. As the customs
officer cannot understand the language Mr Dziekanski is
speaking, he uses a leaflet for identifying the language of
arriving passengers. Once he establishes that Mr Dziekanski is
Polish, the officer provides him with Polish language
instructions for filling out customs declarations cards.

It is reported that Robert then takes an unusually long time to
complete the form, repeatedly mopping his brow with a
handkerchief.

Eventually he returns to the customs booth, clears primary inspection, and is advanced to further processing.

Between 16:09 and 19:00, Robert's whereabouts remain unknown. During this time he would have been unable to leave the secure area.

At around 18:50, Robert's mother, who has now been waiting for over three hours, approaches a help counter on the departures level. Although she is unable to provide precise information on the airline, flight number, or originating city of Robert's flight, two announcements are made over the public address system.

Mrs Cisowski provides assistance on the pronunciation of Robert Dziekanski's name. She is not told that the announcement will not be heard inside the secure customs hall.

At around 19:15, Mrs Cisowski is directed to the outer immigration area. Her husband uses a public service phone to call the Canadian Border Services Agency. As a result of this call, a border officer verifies the names of those people being detained by immigration. Robert is not among them.

Between 21:29 and 21:31, Robert is captured on security-camera footage walking to the west side of baggage carousel 23 in the customs hall.

At some time after 22:00, Mrs Cisowski and her husband depart from the airport and begin the four-hour journey back to their home in Kamloops.

At 22:35, Mr Dziekanski is sent to secondary inspection after attempting to leave the customs hall. When his passport is examined the border-services officer notices that an immigration visa has not been stamped. A search of Mr Dziekanski's luggage fails to produce the necessary immigration documentation.

At 22:44, two border-services officers escort Mr Dziekanski to immigration.

By 23:15, the officers have retrieved two more pieces of Mr Dziekanski's checked luggage from the Lufthansa baggage counter. They return these bags to Mr Dziekanski.

Between 23:15 and 23:40, while Robert sits in the waiting area, the rest of his documentation is found in his bags and the processing of his immigration begins.

At this time an announcement is made, paging his relatives.

At some time between 23:40 and midnight, the Canadian Border Services Agency telephones Mrs Cisowski's home in Kamloops and leaves a message. Mrs Cisowski has not yet arrived home. Another agent goes to the public waiting area to ask if anyone is waiting for a Polish immigrant.

It is now 14th October 2007.

Thanks to the help of a Canadian border-services officer with a rudimentary knowledge of the Polish language, Robert Dziekanski completes the immigration process and is released.

In the period between 00:15 and 00:39, the Canadian border-services officer with basic Polish notices that Robert has gone back to sitting in the waiting area, and tells him that he is now free to go.

At around 00:40, this agent accompanies Robert into the international reception lounge, out of the controlled customs area.

At precisely 00:53, Robert comes into the meet-and-greet area where he sits on a bench.

At 00:57, Robert pushes his bags on a luggage cart back towards the international reception. A low Plexiglas wall blocks his path.

At 01:05, he lifts his luggage over the Plexiglas wall and onto the walkway in front of the door. He then climbs over the wall and begins to bang on the door of the international reception lounge.

At 01:08, a baggage cart attendant approaches a man banging on the door of the international reception lounge and tells him to calm down. A member of the public also unsuccessfully intervenes.

At 01:13 it is known that Robert Dziekanski returns to the international arrivals lounge with his luggage.

At 01:18, the first call is placed to security about an individual 'making trouble' and 'throwing chairs'. It is at around this time that Robert is recorded by a passenger in the international arrivals lounge. The rest of Robert's life is on this film.

At 01:20, a woman places a second call to security about a man believed to be Russian. She is quoted as saying, 'He is really drunk and is throwing suitcases around.'

At 01:26, a crowd of around fifteen people, including two security guards, observe a drunk and aggressive Russian pick up and throw a computer monitor. He has also placed a small table and two chairs to obstruct the automatic door between international arrivals and the meet-and-greet area. Upon being challenged, he stops for a moment and then continues. There is some dialogue between the man and members of the crowd.

At 01:27, precisely four members of the Royal Canadian Mounted Police arrive in the international arrivals lounge. While still some distance from the man causing the disturbance, one officer is recorded on the soundtrack of the video, saying, 'Can I Taser him?' The instant reply is 'Yup.'

Four officers approach the man, members of the crowd inform them that he speaks no English. One of them instructs him, 'Calm down, just calm down.' Lifting his hands above his head, the man causing the disturbance walks backwards, he carries something in his hand. Twenty-four seconds later he is hit with a 50,000-volt shock from a Taser.

01:28. After falling to the floor, the man is hit with the second shock from a Taser. From his hand he drops an object, later identified as a stapler.

01:31 to 01:39. After being strenuously restrained, the man is placed in the recovery position. In their report, the Royal Canadian Mounted Police state that Mr Dziekanski's vital signs were checked repeatedly and that he had a pulse and was still breathing. These actions are not evident from the video.

01:42. An ambulance arrives.

01:44 to 02:10. Paramedics perform CPR on Mr Dziekanski.

At 10 past 2 in the morning, Mrs Cisowski arrives at her home in Kamloops. She receives the message left by the Canadian Border Services Agency and returns the call. The agent with rudimentary Polish tells her that her son did arrive, that he had taken a long time to clear customs and immigration, that he had helped Robert, and that at the end of the shift he would look for him and bring him to the office to call her. The officer is unaware of what was happening in the international lounge.

02:20. Robert Dziekanski is declared dead.

**Transcript of Video at Toronto Airport**

*The following is a transcript of sound from the video shot at the airport.*

- What language do you speak?

- Look at his face.

- There is 300 people coming in, at least coming in...

  *Muffled voices.*

- He almost threw the chair through the window... look at him.

- He is on the other side.

- Look at his face.

  *Heavy breathing by Robert Dziekanski.*

- I can't believe he's sticking his tongue out.

- There is nobody here.

- Five minutes before Cathay comes down with 300 people on it and...

- (*Dziekanski holds a small wooden table and waves it. In Polish:*) Fuck! I will not let you accuse me of anything.

- There is something wrong with him.

- I think he speaks Russian, Russian.

- Is that what he is speaking?

- He doesn't even speak English.

- What language do you speak?

- Russian, Russian.

- Yugoslavian.

- I think he speaks Russian, Russian.

- There is nothing wrong, there is nothing wrong.

- Russian, Russian.

- We need a Russian interpreter.

- Calm down. (*Woman approaches and holds out her hand to try to communicate*.) Excuse me… I'm just going to talk with you… Easy, easy, I know, I know… easy, easy.

- I'd be afraid.

- I told him that.

- He is freaking out.

    *Dziekanski, agitated, picks up a computer.*

- Look at that, he's got a computer.

- Oh!

- Right in front of the cops, too.

- Breaking computers.

    *Dziekanski throws a chair through the glass.*

- There goes the glass.

- Jesus Christ.

- Sir, sir.

- No, no, no, no.

- Oh my God, no.

- (*Crowd member calls to woman who has approached Dziekanski, trying to get her to come back from a window near him*.) Ma'am!

- He speaks Russian and nobody can help him, we need a Russian interpreter here to calm him down.

- There is 300 people coming in.

- He is so scared, why do they just leave him?

- Why are the police not here?

- Did you call security?… Did you call the police?

- Yes, I am at the airport.

- The keyboard he is holding in security.

  *Police arrive in the international arrivals area.*

- What are you doing? What are you doing?

- He is right inside here on the other side of the door.

- (*Dziekanski screams in Polish:*) Police, police.

- He speaks Russian.

- He is freaking out.

- Sir, he speaks Russian, that's it, no English.

  *Police approach Dziekanski. Dziekanski starts backing away, raising his arms briefly. A few moments later he starts screaming. He holds his arm, moaning in pain. He falls to the ground. He screams repeatedly.*

- Jesus Christ.

  *Dziekanski is pinned on the ground by four RCMP officers. He struggles, kicking his feet.*

- It's sad.

- How is he still fighting them off?

- He is still freaking out.

- Nobody knows why.

- He speaks Russian.

- No rhyme or reason.

- Prime footage for my home videos.

- I'm at an airport, man.

- I came in here...

- Is he unconscious?

- Is he dead?

- I heard them say 'code red'?

- Well, yeah.

- I have three minutes of footage left... I have three minutes of memory left, I have three minutes of memory left.


*At the time of going to press, the video is available to view at http://www.youtube.com/watch?v=IPe_hf7aBXM*

**A Nick Hern Book**

*Cherry Blossom* first published in Great Britain as a paperback original in 2008 by Nick Hern Books Limited, 14 Larden Road, London W3 7ST, in association with the Traverse Theatre, Edinburgh, and Teatr Polski, Bydgoszcz, Poland

*Cherry Blossom* copyright © 2008 Catherine Grosvenor

Catherine Grosvenor has asserted her right to be identified as the author of this work

Quotes in Scene Twenty-One included with kind permission from the Private Rented Housing Panel (PRHP)

Cover image: Teatr Polski, Bydgoszcz
Cover design: Ned Hoste, 2H

Typeset by Nick Hern Books, London
Printed and bound in Great Britain by
CPI Antony Rowe, Chippenham, Wiltshire

A CIP catalogue record for this book is available from the British Library

ISBN 978 1 84842 003 8